Will I Find Faith
Christianity at a Crossroads

Fred Snowden

Will I Find Faith?
Copyright © 2020 by Fred Snowden

All rights reserved. No part of this publication may be reproduced, distributed, or transmitted in any form or by any means, including photocopying, recording, or other electronic or mechanical methods, without the prior written permission of the publisher or author, except in the case of brief quotations embodied in critical reviews and certain other noncommercial uses permitted by copyright law.

Although every precaution has been taken to verify the accuracy of the information contained herein, the author and publisher assume no responsibility for any errors or omissions. No liability is assumed for damages that may result from the use of information contained within.

Library of Congress Control Number: 2020909520
ISBN-13:   Paperback: 978-1-64749-122-2

Printed in the United States of America

GoToPublish LLC
1-888-337-1724
www.gotopublish.com
info@gotopublish.com

CONTENTS

FOREWORD vii
CHAPTER ONE – WHAT IS FAITH? 1
CHAPTER 2 – AMERICA'S MORAL DECLINE 17
CHAPTER 3 – FREEDOM OF RELIGION
   HAS BECOME FREEDOM FROM RELIGION 29
CHAPTER 4– THE AMERICAN CHURCH IS IN
   RETREAT 47
CHAPTER 5 – HOLLYWOOD & THE MEDIA ARE
   WINNING THE BATTLE OF INFLUENCE 59
CHAPTER 6- 21ST CENTURY AMERICA HAS
   BECOME 4TH CENTURY ROME 65
PROLOGUE 73

FOREWORD

I have always wondered what Jesus intended when he asked, "Will the Son of Man find faith on the Earth when he returns"? (Luke 18:8). That is a daunting question, one that all Christians and even unbelievers should want to understand. Nearly one billion people on earth call themselves Christian, 250 million in the United States alone, and it seems that Christianity is still growing. So, shouldn't the answer be obvious?

Maybe so, but possibly not. The key to understanding Jesus' question and the possible contradictions between the obvious and subtle are in understanding what Jesus meant by the word "faith". A consideration of the whole of His teachings indicates that the faith He is speaking of is saving faith; faith which is required to be born again, to become Jesus' disciple. Most of us would simply call this the faith that is required to become a Christian. Jesus described this kind of faith in detail to Nicodemus in John 3; some would say the most important chapter in all the Bible.

Many people who are born into a Christian home, even in a post-Christian nation like America, find it convenient to identify themselves as Christian; especially those whose parents or grandparents call themselves Christians. I meet people every day who say they are Christians, but what they mean is that they are not atheists and are good, religious people. They assume that being a good religious person is the same thing as being a Christian. The Pharisees of Jesus' day were good religious people, but they were Jesus' greatest critics and He theirs.

It may seem contradictory but being religious can actually be antithetical to becoming a Christian. Religious people are kind to animals, hold the door for the elderly, go to church on special holidays, support the Red Cross, are good neighbors, may be members of a

Christian church, organization or club and have their infant children baptized. So, isn't that a Christian? According to Jesus, it is not!

CHAPTER ONE – WHAT IS FAITH?

Jesus, the founder of our faith, provided for us specific, measurable instructions for becoming His follower. In a night meeting with a Pharisee, Nikodemus, He provided detailed instruction on becoming a Christian. John tells us of their conversation:

John 3: 1-16

> *3Now there was a Pharisee, a man named Nicodemus who was a member of the Jewish ruling council. 2 He came to Jesus at night and said, "Rabbi, we know that you are a teacher who has come from God. For no one could perform the signs you are doing if God were not with him."*
>
> *3 Jesus replied, "Very truly I tell you, no one can see the kingdom of God unless they are born again."*
>
> *4 "How can someone be born when they are old?" Nicodemus asked. "Surely they cannot enter a second time into their mother's womb to be born!"*
>
> *5 Jesus answered, "Very truly I tell you, no one can enter the kingdom of God unless they are born of water and the Spirit. 6 Flesh gives birth to flesh, but the Spirit[b] gives birth to spirit. 7 You should not be surprised at my saying, 'You[c] must be born again.' 8 The wind blows wherever it pleases. You hear its sound, but you cannot tell where it comes from or where it is going. So it is with everyone born of the Spirit."[d]*
>
> *9 "How can this be?" Nicodemus asked.*
>
> *10"You are Israel's teacher," said Jesus, "and do you not understand these things? 11 Very truly I tell you, we speak of what we know, and we testify to what we have seen, but still you people do not accept our testimony. 12 I have spoken to you of earthly things and you do not believe; how then will you*

> believe if I speak of heavenly things? *¹³* No one has ever gone into heaven except the one who came from heaven—the Son of Man,[e] *¹⁴* Just as Moses lifted up the snake in the wilderness, so the Son of Man must be lifted up,[f] *¹⁵* that everyone who believes may have eternal life in him."
>
> *¹⁶* For God so loved the world that he gave his one and only Son, that whoever believes in him shall not perish but have eternal life. *¹⁷* For God did not send his Son into the world to condemn the world, but to save the world through him. *¹⁸* Whoever believes in him is not condemned, but whoever does not believe stands condemned already because they have not believed in the name of God's one and only Son. *¹⁹* This is the verdict: Light has come into the world, but people loved darkness instead of light because their deeds were evil. *²⁰* Everyone who does evil hates the light and will not come into the light for fear that their deeds will be exposed. *²¹* But whoever lives by the truth comes into the light, so that it may be seen plainly that what they have done has been done in the sight of God.

This might be the most preached and least understood section of scripture of all time and the truth is; one either gets it or doesn't. An elderly Puerto Rican man carefully explained these scriptures to me when I was 12 years old and I just didn't get it, but two years later, after God had time to work in my heart, I finally got it! One moment I was a sinner, the next I was a believer. One moment I had no relationship with God, the next we were intimate friends. One moment, I had no hope for the future, the next I was overwhelmed with expectation and hope.

By the way, when I was 12, I would have told you I was a Christian because my mother had me baptised in the Catholic Church and I thought I was a follower of Christ. Later, she was excommunicated from the church for divorcing my father and we never attended church again. When I started high school, I felt very empty. Success in football, academics and relationships that I thought would bring satisfaction, just didn't. I decided to see why church was important to some of my friends. A nearby church had visited our home to invite us to attend, so we decided to give it a try. I am so thankful that it was a Gospel preaching church. The sermon I heard that day was not taken from John 3, but the message of John 3:16 was woven throughout the passionate preaching.

We know that Nikodemus "got it" because he braved the might of Rome, asked Pilate for Jesus' dead body, and buried the Lord's body in his own tomb; temporarily I might add. But, we do not know when he got it…was it that night when he first spoke with Jesus, was it when he saw a leper healed, was it when he saw 5,000 families fed with a boys lunch, was it when he observed Jesus on the cross saying, "Father forgive them for they know not what they do"? We know that Nicodemus became a Christian because it was evidenced in his behavior, but we cannot say exactly when.

Before returning to my topic, allow me to make 3 comments about the somewhat confusing simile found John 3:

1. Verses 6-7 are the key to understanding what Jesus meant about being born again.

   "Flesh gives birth to flesh, but the Spirit gives birth to spirit. The wind blows wherever it pleases. You hear its sound, but you cannot tell where it comes from or where it is going. So, it is with everyone born of the Spirit."

   One can only become a Christian through the intervention and working of the Spirit of God. Going to church is not enough, doing good works is not enough, being born into a Christian home is not enough, saying a prayer at an altar is not enough. Salvation requires that the Holy Spirit convict us to bring us to the point of genuine repentance and His tender touch to assist us in exercising saving faith in Jesus' finished work on the cross. The spiritual New Birth is accomplished only in and through the Holy Spirit. We are saved through God's grace, when He, the Holy Spirit, moves upon our heart and draws us to Jesus. If unusual things are happening in your life, it may be the Holy Spirit working to bring you to the point where you can be born again as a child of God. Paul put it this way in his letter to the Church in Rome (chapter 8, verses 15-16);

   15So you have not received a spirit that makes you fearful slaves. Instead, you received God's Spirit when he adopted you as his own children. Now we call him, "Abba, Father."i 16For his Spirit joins with our spirit to affirm that we are God's children.

2. The new birth is an allegory or simile of our natural birth.

　　When we were born physically, our mothers oozed both water and blood. In the spiritual new birth, the same two elements are present; the blood of Christ, shed to take the punishment we deserved for sin and the water and blood that oozed from His *broken heart when it was pierced by the soldier's spear. Coming to Christ is no casual experience, it is a gut-wrenching, life-changing, overwhelming experience like our natural birth. When one breathes the first breath of air, after repenting and receiving Christ as Lord and Savior, change is apparent.

　　I Peter 1:18, For you know that it was not with perishable things such as silver or gold that you were redeemed from the empty way of life handed down to you from your ancestors, but with the precious blood of Christ, a lamb without blemish or defect.

3. Salvation can only come after you understand and practice the illustration Jesus offered in verse 14. Nicodemus would have been very familiar with this illustration, but some readers may not be. Since this illustration is vital to understanding what true conversion is and is not, we must believe what Jesus said.

　　14 Just as Moses lifted up the snake in the wilderness, so the Son of Man must be lifted up, 15 that everyone who believes may have eternal life in him.

During wilderness wanderings of the Jews, after their release from Egyptian slavery and subsequent refusal to enter the Promised Land, God sent numerous trials to mature them and condition them to possess the land some 40 years later. The first of these trials, which is described in Numbers, chapter 9, was poisonous snakes invading the camp. People who were bitten by these serpents died, so the people began to repent and cry out to Moses for deliverance. The seemingly obtuse remedy God gave was to have Moses hang the brazen image of a snake on a high pole in the middle of the encampment. Any who were bitten could go to this pole, look up at the image of the snake and live. There is an old hymn written by William Ogden in 1887, "Look and Live" that aligns the Old Testament story with Jesus crucifixion and resurrection.

Refrain:
"Look and live,"

my brother, live,Look to Jesus now, and live;
'Tis recorded in His word, hallelujah!
It is only that you "look and live."

Something this passage does not address is if everyone who was bitten accepted the remedy God provided. As a pastor of 45 years, I expect not. Salvation is offered free today to everyone who will be born again, yet many decide, like Frank Sinatra and Cain, to "do it their own way". So, those who were bitten that tried an herb potion died, those who used a drawing compress died, those who prayed to God for healing died, those who improved their behavior died. Only those who expressed saving faith in the remedy God provided, came to the foot of the pole and looked upon the brass serpent were saved.

Jesus was telling Nicodemus that the day would come when He would be lifted-up towards heaven on a cruel Roman cross and that only those who dared look upon that sacrifice and accept it by faith, as the only means of salvation, would be saved. Do you believe God's Word? Have you come to the foot of the cross and gazed upon the bloodied, broken body of Jesus? Do you understand that there is no other way to be delivered from sin and death than the cross of Christ? If so, you are a Christian or you are ready to become one right now. If not, you are lost and hopeless.

> ...looking to Jesus, the founder and perfecter of our faith, who for the joy that was set before Him endured the cross, despising the shame, and is seated at the right hand of the throne of God.
> Hebrews $^{12:2}$

This illustration speaks to the sacrifices of Cain and Able, which are recorded in Genesis chapter 4. Able brought a slain lamb; Cain brought a beautiful cornucopia. One expressed a great deal of talent and effort; the other simple faith. The logical context of this story is that, like Able, Cain knew what sacrifice God demanded, but decided to offer the work of his own hands. This is the problem with today's generation. We know that God demands faith and obedience, but we want to offer something other than that and hope God will accept it.

If you are not a believer now, it may not be entirely your fault. We, the supposed followers of Jesus, have not done very well in attracting and making disciples. We have done better with getting unbelievers to come to church and attend classes and groups. Unfortunately, we have done a horrible job of helping people to walk as Jesus walked, talk as Jesus talked and make genuine disciples as Jesus did.

The way we know that Jesus accomplished His mission, as He defined it in Matthew 28:19-20, is that His disciples made new disciples: Peter – Mark & Barnabas; John – Polycarp and Ignatius; Paul – Luke, Timothy and Titus. These second-generation disciples were the genuine article and carried on the work of making disciples as did the Apostles. If that process of disciple-making had continued as intended, we would not be where we find ourselves in the 21st Century.

Many of us, who had good intentions, may have unintentionally mishandled the mission by offending you or leading you down a path that did not lead to your genuine conversion. Thank God, there is still an opportunity for you to follow Nicodemus' example. American Christianity is in crisis because we have not helped people to be born again and made to become disciples. Nor have we adequately and effectively confronted our nation's spiritual and resulting moral decline. Our neglect of duty and silence is unforgivable.

As a result of our failure, I believe that the statistics given in the foreword for the number of Christians in the US are vastly exaggerated. I estimate that one-half or fewer of the estimated 250M Christians is more accurate, and I am concerned that the numbers will continue to decline as we enter a period when Christ's followers will experience genuine persecution. I hope that I am wrong, but the information I present later, of the currently escalating moral decline of our culture, supports this unfortunate assertion.

Maybe you are uncertain of your own relationship status with God. If so, there are three ways to evaluate your life to know if you are truly a follower of Jesus. These are not the rules for becoming a Christian. We are saved by grace and grace alone and nothing that we do or say can save us.

> *Ephesians $2{:}8\text{-}9$ (KJV) ^{8} For by grace are ye saved through faith; and that not of yourselves: it is the gift of God: ^{9} Not of works, lest any man should boast.*

It is only through the blood of Christ that we can be forgiven, but these three criteria may help you see if you are following Christ and making progress in your Christian walk.

OBEDIENCE

Simply put, genuine believers live in obedience to God's Word. As Christ's disciples, we obey the Ten Commandments and the remainder of the moral law revealed in the Old Testament. We are not bound to the dietary, political and ceremonial portions of that Law and obeying the moral Law in no way saves us or makes us more deserving of God's grace. But the moral law is the very revelation of God's nature and God commands us to "be holy as I am is holy". Being a rebellious law breaker does not please God. James, Jesus' brother reminded us,

"For whosoever shall keep the whole law, and yet offend in one point, he is guilty of all." James $2^{:10}$

Furthermore, in keeping the 10 Commandments, we observe Jesus' Two Great Commandments, which are a summation of the Ten.

Jesus replied: "Love the Lord your God with all your heart and with all your soul and with all your mind. This is the first and greatest commandment. And the second is like it: Love your neighbor as yourself." Matthew $22^{:37}$-^{39}

If you have heard a modernist pastor say we are not obligated to the Law, he/she is deceiving you as is pointed out by the Apostle Paul:

Do you not know that the wicked will not inherit the kingdom of God? Do not be deceived: Neither the sexually immoral, nor idolaters, nor adulterers, nor men who submit to or perform homosexual acts, [10] *nor thieves, nor the greedy, nor drunkards, nor verbal abusers, nor swindlers, will inherit the kingdom of God....*I Corinthians $6^{: 9}$

If he/she said that keeping the law will not save you, that is correct. Once again, we are saved through the unmerited love and favor of God by exercising faith in the finished work of Christ on the cross, but once we are saved, we want to obey all of God's commandments and everything else He says in His Word. Christians love and obey the Lord unconditionally, in good times and bad, love their neighbors, do no evil or think no evil towards them, follow the admonitions of scripture and our spiritual leaders as long as they are following Jesus. The acid test in respect to today's corrupting society is that genuine Christians, who would be disciples, make disciples and influence the culture for good and for God. We...

- Do good works; not to earn salvation, but it is a natural and normal outflow of Christ's indwelling.
- *For we are his workmanship, created in Christ Jesus for good works.* Ephesians 2:10 ESV
- Do not abuse alcohol or drugs.

    ...and do not get drunk with wine, for that is debauchery, but be filled with the spirit... Ephesians 5:14 ESV

- Do not engage in any pre-marital or extra-marital sex of any kind, including viewing pornography, which Jesus called as adultery.

    "The body is not meant for sexual immorality, but for the Lord...flee fornication...he that commits fornication sins against his body. What? Don't you know that your body is the Temple of the Holy Spirit...therefore; glorify God in your body and in your spirit, which are God's." I Corinthians 6:[13]b, [18]-[20]

- Do not to divorce or cause harm to our spouse or family in any way. Jesus allowed two exceptions for adultery, (adultery and desertion) but in cases where spouses are willing to repent, the offending partner can be forgiven by God and their spouse, and the broken marriage can be restored. Remember that Christian marriage is a picture to the world of the relationship that exists between Christ and His bride, the Church and is sacred.

    [3] Some Pharisees came to him to test him. They asked, "Is it lawful for a man to divorce his wife for any and every reason?" [4] "Haven't you read," he replied, "that at the beginning the Creator 'made them male and female,[a] [5] and said, 'For this reason a man will leave his father and mother and be united to his wife, and the two will become one flesh[b]'? [6] So they are no longer two, but one flesh. Therefore what God has joined together, let no one separate." [7] "Why then," they asked, "did Moses command that a man give his wife a certificate of divorce and send her away?" [8] Jesus replied, "Moses permitted you to divorce your wives because your hearts were hard. But it was not this way from the beginning. [9] I tell you that

anyone who divorces his wife, except for sexual immorality, and marries another woman commits adultery." Matthew 19:3-12 (NIV)

- Do not condone abortion or infanticide, but have tender, compassionate hearts towards women with an unwanted pregnancy and help them find options other than abortion.

    [13] For you created my inmost being you knit me together in my mother's womb. [14] I praise you because I am fearfully and wonderfully made; your works are wonderful; I know that full well. [15] My frame was not hidden from you when I was made in the secret place, when I was woven together in the depths of the earth. [16] Your eyes saw my unformed body; all the days ordained for me were written in your book before one of them came to be. Proverbs 139:13-16

    "Before I formed you in the womb, I knew you, and before you were born, I consecrated you; I appointed you a prophet to the nations." Jeremiah 1:5 ESV

- Understand that our wealth belongs to God and give significant amounts of your resources to support the work of God.

    Honor the LORD with your wealth and with the best part of everything you produce. Proverbs 3:9

    Have I ever failed to obey any of these things? You bet, and you have too! But when we sin, there is forgiveness in Christ. The objective is to obey and not sin, but if we do sin, there is forgiveness through Christ's atoning blood.

    "My little children, these things write I unto you, that ye sin not. And if any man sin, we have an advocate with the Father, Jesus Christ the righteous; and he is the atoning sacrifice for our sins, and not for ours only, but also for the whole world. This is how we know that we know him: if we keep his commandments.
    I John 2:1-3

Can we keep sinning continually and be a Christian? No! Even though we know that God is merciful and full of Grace, true believers do not to live in habitual sin and failure. If you find yourself living in sin and never having victory over sin, you may be one of those who Jesus spoke of in the Parable of the Sower, in Matthew 13:1-23. He said that some of the seed fell on those whose heart was rocky and the seed (the Word of God) never took good root. If that is the case, there is still abundant mercy and forgiveness waiting for you. Repent, be truly sorry for and turn from sin, receive Jesus' forgiveness and make Him your Lord (pilot, not co-pilot). Read the Word every day, pray, find a church in which you can be discipled, make new Christian friends and become solid and mature in your faith. Being a Christian requires commitment and discipline; it changes our lives from the inside out as we follow Jesus and give him complete control of our being.

"Be ye not conformed to this world but be ye transformed by the renewing of your mind...Romans 12:2

GROWTH

Babies grow through the sustenance of milk. New believers grow through spiritual sustenance, found in God's Word.

As newborn babes, desire the sincere milk of the word, that ye may grow thereby... I Peter 2:2

The Bible can be hard to understand for a non-believer, but the pages of scripture come alive for believers. During 45 years as a pastor, hundreds of new converts have told me that "the scriptures began to jump off the page at me" after accepting Christ. Studying God's Word is a necessary discipline for Christ's disciple. It informs, warns, corrects, inspires, comforts, admonishes and exhorts. According to my Bahamian friend, Miles Monroe, "it is the Constitution of the Kingdom of God".

During the two years between first hearing the Gospel and receiving it, I read the Bible a lot, so much that people assumed I was a Christian. In fact, I read it from cover to cover; twice. When I became a Christian, it was familiar, but the Word became so much more alive, poignant and meaningful. I fell in love with God's Word and it was nothing for me to study the Bible for 2-3 hours a day. I loved it and I literally felt the growth, not just in understanding, but growth in obedience, character and in the fruits of the Spirit.

Most importantly, the constant "washing of the Word" was healthy. The importance of the Word in a believer's life cannot be overstated. Reading and studying the Bible every day is essential to sustainable growth. My experience is that when we stop growing, we start shrinking.

If you have an insatiable hunger for God's Word, you are a Christian or close to becoming one. Jesus first wilderness temptation was to turn a stone into a loaf of bread, He would not and told Satan. "man does not live by bread alone, but by every word the Father speaks" So, do not neglect the Bread of Life.

I might add the importance of prayer, but it is impossible not to talk to God when you are intently studying the Word. The two disciplines are inseparable, but not always equal in practice or effectiveness.

PRODUCE FRUIT

The fruit of a pear tree is a pear. The fruit of Jesus' disciple is another disciple.

> Matthew ^{28}: ^{19}-^{20} *Go therefore and make disciples of all the nations, baptizing them to the name of the Father, and of the Son, and of the Holy Spirit; teaching them to observe all things whatsoever I have taught you.*

This was not spoken to pastors, evangelists and missionaries, but ordinary believers like you and me. This is a command and as we learned in the previous sections true believers obey Christs commands. If you are bringing others to the Lord and instructing them in the ways of the Lord, you are producing fruit.

Then, there are also the fruits of the Spirit that demonstrate that we are day by day being conformed into the image of Jesus.: Galatians 5:22-23

> *But the Holy Spirit produces this kind of fruit in our lives: love, joy, peace, patience, kindness, goodness, faithfulness, gentleness, and self-control. There is no law against these things!*

These are the attributes that flow from the new nature of a new believer. As a newborn infant, our new Christ-life overcomes the old.

> *This means that anyone who belongs to Christ has become a new person. The old life is gone; a new life has begun! II Corinthians $^{5:17}$*

These fruits of the Spirit are observable and measurable. When a believer is growing in the Word, living in obedience, reproducing regularly, the fruit harvest is bountiful. When there is failure in any of these areas, not so much. By the way, it takes time to grow fruit. From the time a vineyard is first planted, it may take 5 years to produce the first bottle of wine. Thankfully, God is patient and long-suffering. Unfortunately, people are not!

The key to being fruitful is remaining connected to the vine.

John 15:1-8 New International Version (NIV)

> [15] "I am the true vine, and my Father is the gardener. [2] He cuts off every branch in me that bears no fruit, while every branch that does bear fruit he prunes[a] so that it will be even more fruitful. [3] You are already clean because of the word I have spoken to you. [4] Remain in me, as I also remain in you. No branch can bear fruit by itself; it must remain in the vine. Neither can you bear fruit unless you remain in me. [5] "I am the vine; you are the branches. If you remain in me and I in you, you will bear much fruit; apart from me you can do nothing. [6] If you do not remain in me, you are like a branch that is thrown away and withers; such branches are picked up, thrown into the fire and burned.

This is simply understood; and easily done. Stay connected to Jesus! If something comes between you and the Lord, turn away from it immediately, repent and dig in again. When he prunes you back, take it and be thankful. Don't take your eyes off Jesus, not for a moment. As you abide in Him, His life will flow through you, cleanse you, give new life to you, empower you and keep you from failure.

The point I have been making is that being a Christian requires far more engagement than simply saying one is a Christian; it means more than repeating a prayer and returning to one's old life. Over the last few decades, our culture has deteriorated so fast that it is difficult to recognize who is a Christian and who is not, but God knows; he sees our hearts. On the other hand, one could outwardly follow the evidences I described above and still not have faith. Unless we repent, confess Jesus as Lord and received His death, burial and resurrection alone for salvation, behavior is inconsequential. Christ alone saves, a changed life is a product of His Lordship and the indwelling of the Holy Spirit. Paul put it this way:

> I have been crucified with Christ and I no longer live, but Christ lives in me. The life I now live in the body, I live by

faith in the Son of God, who loved me and gave himself for me. Galatians 2:20

Some of you may think that the lifestyle I have described is "harsh, judgmental and legalistic", but there are hundreds of ministries that remain true to the Bible and the Gospel message as delivered to the Apostles, and are conveying a similar message: John MacArthur, Michael Youssef, Focus on the Family, Family Life Today, Franklin Graham, Bob Jones University, Pensacola Christian College, Gary Hamrick, Alistair Begg, Jerry Falwell, Jr., Jerry Vines and Robert Jeffress, uust to name a few.. The problem is that there are 100,000 churches preaching a watered down, ineffective, powerless gospel for every one that remains faithful to the Gospel that changes lives and produces genuine disciples.

Some might ask, is there precedent for strong Christian nations becoming secularized and/or paganized? There certainly is and Egypt was the first. After becoming a leading Christian center in the Roman Empire, it was conquered by the **Rashidun Caliphate** in 639 BC and Christianity was all but extinguished. Through the Middle Ages, this happened time and and time again as the Muslin armies conquered vast territories in the middle east, Asia, Africa and Europe. Had not Charlemagne's grandfather, Charles Martel, defeated the Muslim invaders at Tours in 732 AD, all of Europe might be controlled by Islam. As Christianity fades in America, Islam will fill the void. For all we see and hear about radical Islam, which is more political than spiritual, Muslims are generally respectful, honest, family focused, morally conscientious people, who stand in opposition to the moral corruption that is overtaking American culture.

In more modern times, the best example of a thoroughly Christian nation becoming secularized is Holland. Holland thrived in Europe's Calvinistic Reformation. It became a safe haven for Europe's persecuted Protestants. Our Pilgrim Fathers fled to Holland first before journeying on to Massachusetts. The Dutch Reformed Church was a strong spiritual force in Holland, and later in America and in other parts of the world.

Calvinism, named for the brilliant evangelist and scholar John Calvin, arrived in the Netherlands in the 1540s, converting both parts of the elite and the common population. The Spanish government, under Philip II started harsh persecution campaigns, supported by the Inquisition. In reaction to this persecution, the Calvinists rebelled. In

1566 William the Silent, Prince of Orange, a convert to Calvinism and started the Eighty Years' War to liberate the Calvinist Dutch from the Catholic Spaniards. A considerable number of people were Calvinist by that time. All churches in the Calvinist territories became Calvinist and most of the population in these territories converted to Calvinism. During the 17th century, the larger western cities received an influx of Protestant immigrants from Germany, Flanders, England and France an even more developed Protestant character emerged. Netherlands was ruled by a liberal Calvinist elite, which dominated the bureaucracy and the Dutch Reformed Church.

Today Holland still bears the marks of a Christian nation but less than 10% of the population are practicing Christians. The immorality in Amsterdam is the worst in Europe; nude women sit in store windows, waiting to be purchased for sexual toys, So, could what happened in Egypt and Holland happen in America? Sarah Bailey says it already is happening:

> "Christianity is on the decline in America, not just among younger generations or in certain regions of the country but across race, gender, education and geographic barriers. The percentage of adults who describe themselves as Christians dropped by nearly eight percentage points in just seven years to about [71] percent, according to a survey conducted by the Pew Research Center.
>
> "It's remarkably widespread," said Alan Cooperman, director of religion research for the Pew Research Center. "The country is becoming less religious as a whole, and it's happening across the board." At the same time, the share of those who are not affiliated with a religion has jumped from [16] percent to about [23] percent in the same time period.

So back to the question our Lord asked...

I do believe that Jesus will find faith on the Earth when He returns, but not in America, if our country even exists. Faith may be found in South Korea, the Bahamas, China, Angola, Liberia, Scotland, Bulgaria and Poland, but not in much of the western world. So, now that you are calling me an alarmist or worse, please allow me to reveal the chapter titles that follow, and which form the premise for the collapse of Christianity in America:

- America's Moral Decline
- Freedom of Religion has Become Freedom from Religion
- The American Church is in Retreat
- Hollywood and the Main-stream Media are winning the War of Influence
- 21st Century America has Become 4th Century Rome

This disclaimer before proceeding; the problem in American culture is not moral decadence. It is the lack of genuinely converted Christians, who are committed to being salt and light in our culture. The former is symptomatic of the later, but who is to blame for that? Me, other believers and the clueless Christian church in America. Winning the lost is our responsibility, our prime directive, and we have failed miserably. It seems that reaching the lost has been our lowest priority. We have been complacent, neglectful, disobedient and uncompassionate. Our failure to introduce our culture to the Jesus of the Bible has made America what she is today. Non-believers are not to blame for America's moral decline, since amorality is the natural product of an unredeemed life, one that lacks an example to emulate.

Although many would contend that the church is not responsible for the promotion of any political agenda, in the absence of evangelism, the church might have addressed the important moral issues that face contemporary culture more effectively. But, like ostriches with our heads in the sand, we have failed throughout the scope of our nation's history to get it right. Were have been asleep at the wheel when

*The Slavery Clause was removed from the Declaration of Independence

*When slavery was not abolished by our new Constitution? (adoption of the 3/5ths Compromise, totally disenfranchised Africans and normalized slavery)

When Andrew Jackson, and other of our presidents and congressional leaders, waged an unholy, unjust war against the native Americans

When the Jim Crow laws were introduced

When America rescinded Prohibition rather than fighting racketeering

When Bible reading and prayer were removed from public schools

When Roe v Wade became the law of the land

When marriage was redefined by the government

When marijuana was legalized and/or decriminalized

Since we failed to reach our nation with the Gospel, the least we could have done is to stick our fingers into the holes in the dam of moral decline. We did neither, so our failure is compounded, and we find our culture in moral chaos.

> *Slavery and segregation forever marginalized the influence of Christianity in America. A lack of scholarship and intentionally biased misinterpretation of scriptures found in Ephesians, chapter 6, Philemon and other New Testament passages are unforgivable. Historical and Cultural context are the keys to discovering the 'then and there' meaning of scripture that gives clarity to the 'here and now' interpretation. Roman slavery, of which Paul wrote, was entirely different than the horrible, cruel, dehumanizing brand of slavery bequeathed to us by the Spanish and British. This misinterpreted scriptural support for bondage kept slavery alive in much of the US until President Lincoln's Emancipation Proclamation. The contributions to the abolition of slavery by northern Christians and entire Christian denominations often goes overlooked, which is understandable, given the failure of so many shallow, selfish Christians who turned their backs on their brothers and sisters. The fact that such a great number of the formerly enslaved in America responded to Christ and followed Him is a testimony to the sovereignty and grace of God. Unfortunately, a great divide still exists between the black and white church today. It has been said that Sunday mornings are the most segregated time in America. Having served a predominantly African American church for eighteen years, I can say unequivocally that leading people who come from an experience of mistreatment, abuse and condescension are much more spiritually sensitive and passionate.

CHAPTER 2 – AMERICA'S MORAL DECLINE

In Paul's second letter to his disciple and go-to guy, Timothy, we find this warning in chapter 3, verses 1-5:

> [1] But mark this: There will be terrible times in the last days. [2] People will be lovers of themselves, lovers of money, boastful, proud, abusive, disobedient to their parents, ungrateful, unholy, [3] without love, unforgiving, slanderous, without self-control, brutal, not lovers of the good, [4] treacherous, rash, conceited, lovers of pleasure rather than lovers of God— [5] having a form of godliness but denying its power. Have nothing to do with such people.

No doubt, we are witnessing in the 21st Century in America what is being described in this prophecy. There has never been such thing as a "Christian Nation", but there are nations that are Christian in nature and in which the vast majority of citizens are devoted to Christ. I grew up in such a nation; America, during the 1950s. And make no mistake, at that time in history, President Obama would have been wrong if he said, "America is not a Christian nation".

Not that everyone was a Christian, but the Judeo-Christian ethic dominated the landscape. There were still honkey-tonks, houses of ill repute, gangsters and miscreants, but they were hidden, for the most part, certainly not tolerated or celebrated by society, and they were subject to justice that was swift and sure. Back then, not even the smallest infraction got by our Sheriff and his diligent deputies.

The government, media, schools and public institutions sang the same tune, something akin to "God Bless America". The majority of people worked hard, were devoted to their family, were passionate about American exceptionalism and shared the American dream. My mother and father, and others like them from "The Greatest Generation", had survived the Great Depression, won WWII and what most of them wanted was an opportunity for a better life than their parents enjoyed and an even better future for their children.

I grew up in a non-religious, secular home, but even so, Christianity invaded every area of my life. Without fail, my teachers in public schools read the scriptures to us every day and challenged us to obey them. They prayed for us and continually told us that God had a plan for our lives. My baseball coach was a Lutheran pastor, most of my friends went to church and were constantly inviting me to attend church. Even the deputy sheriff who ended my criminal career of filing electric box punchouts to get sodas was a believer who attempted to befriend me and get me under the influence of Christ. It was maddening!

The Ten Commands were proudly displayed in my classrooms, as evidence that America's laws were first God's Law. TV was pure as the driven snow; Ozie and Harriet slept in separate beds, Father always knew best, Cheyenne was a man of integrity and Huntly & Brinkley told the truth. The Lone Ranger was more about Christian virtues than about the wild west and he treated Tonto as an equal. Abortion and sodomy were felonies and were fully prosecuted under the law. The worst R rated movies were equivalent to today's PG films. Pop music was mostly wholesome. Two parent homes were the norm, pregnancy out of wedlock was accommodated but not celebrated, children respected and obeyed their parents and a high percentage of families attended synagogue and church.

My parents' generation handed down the tattered remnants of a healthy moral heritage to my generation. This code had been bequeathed to them from generations past, going all the way back to the Pilgrims. Although, it was never quite as absolute as what the previous generation had passed down, it was still recognizable as Biblical morality. The religious community has not always agreed on everything, but Orthodox Jews, Roman Catholics and Protestants had come together to form the foundation of community consensus on morality that came to be called the Judeo-Christian Ethic. Then, suddenly, in the 1960s, the wheels came off!

The 60s were a decade of incredible change. Peyton Place, The Rolling Stones and Irma La Dulce led the way to a new, relaxed morality. The Arts, ready to throw off the shackles of Puritan bondage, explored the limits of hedonism. The speed of change took on exponential proportions and here we are today. We Boomers may have given the world the space race, the cell phone and the Internet, but we also contributed no-fault divorce, abortion on demand, secularized public schools, legalized marijuana, 21 billion dollars of national debt and nationwide gay marriage.

Early in the 60s, a new elite class arose in the recording industry. Elvis, Johnny Cash, Jerry Lee Lewis. Ray Charles, our teen idols, were alcohol and drug dependent miscreants who used their music and their decadent lifestyles to promote unwholesome values. Actors like James Dean, Bridgett Bardot, Marlon Brando and Norma Jean turned the Hollywood on its head, as films grew increasingly violent and sexually promiscuous. Garage bands and the Rock & Roll revolution exploded on the pages of American history. Money flowed like honey in the Promised Land; Hollywood, Detroit, Memphis and Nashville, as the nuevo-riche artists and filthy rich producers took control of the mainstream media. By 1970, the America I knew had changed irrevocably.

These young social geniuses brilliantly conducted a clandestine anti-morality campaign, as the teens and college students of that day experienced a new world of drugs, free sex and social revolution. The advent of hard rock groups, like the Rolling Stones, accelerated the paradigm shift. Beatles lyrics went from "I want to hold your hand" to "we all live in a yellow submarine", whatever that means. Even the once wholesome Beach Boys, led by the king of drug abuse, Brian Wilson, succumbed. Then came Woodstock!

As time passed and sensibilities eroded, the advent of groups like Kiss openly promoted hedonism, and even Satanism. Although it was "all in good fun", it had a dramatic effect on American culture. Mothers and fathers stood passively by and watched the moral climate erode as they spoiled their precious "Boomers" with the innovative psycho-babel methods of Dr. Spock, not to be confused with Mr. Spock. He put parents on a guilt trip for damaging their children's Ids as corporal punishment became taboo. "Spare the rod and spoil the child" was forgotten and did we ever get spoiled. As we came of age in the late 60s and early 70s, we proudly and aggressively assaulted the tattered remnants of the crumbling Biblical heritage passed down to us by our ancestors. To put it plainly, "America was going to Hell in a Handbasket".

I graduated from high school in the mid-60s when rules were strict: no smoking, tucked-in button-front shirts, no jeans, leather dress shoes, hair off the ears and collar, girls' skirts were to the knees, no excessive make-up, no handholding. In 1970, just a few years after I graduated, I was invited to come back speak at my high school. I was totally blown away by how much things had changed. It was a "brave new world". In the vacuum of Biblical morality, public schools had become the playground of the secular humanist change agents and it showed. As I entered the building, I looked through a sea of long-haired boys, wearing jeans and vulgar T-shirts and braless girls in short skirts and mid-drifts. There was no order whatsoever; chaos reigned and behaviors that would have resulted in my expulsion were the norm. In the distance, saw my principal. He looked at me with a bemused grin. He grimaced and shook his head. Instinctively, I understood; he was no longer in control. The inmates, enabled by their clueless parents, had taken over the institution.

There are many theories for the decline of morality and disintegration of the traditional home in America. No doubt, the seeds were sown long ago with the advent of the Age of Enlightenment, the rise of Darwinian evolution and in the dehumanizing Industrial Revolution. Europe succumbed first and then the millions of American soldiers who fought on the Continent during WWI and WWII had a first-hand experience with moral obscurity. This tolerant, pluralistic, permissive, European society, with relaxed morals and abundant personal freedom, offered an unfettered lifestyle that was embraced by many of our lonely boys, especially in France, Belgium and Holland. Many soldiers, and subsequently their families, were more negatively impacted by European culture than by the horrors of war.

The institution of marriage was the first to suffer. As far as I know, I was the only child in my class throughout elementary school who was the product of divorce, but that began to change rapidly as I entered middle school. The fact is that the divorce rate rose from 8.5% in 1939 to 13.4% by 1969. Today, more than half of all marriages end in divorce. Once marriages began to crumble, the family framework fractured, and the dynamics of the entire culture suffered. Today more homes in America function without a father than with one.

My generation managed to legalize abortion, marijuana and gay marriage, accumulate a $21,000,000,000+ national debt, lose and/or abandon two indistinct and undefined wars, surrender our position as the world's economic leader, set new lows for unemployment, underemployment and home ownership and destroy a moral code that enabled families to form a foundation of strength and stability, which made America a beacon of hope to the rest of the world.

The moral decline has been unabated, although there have been "voices crying in the wilderness": Ruth, Billy and Franklin Graham, Jerry Falwell, James Kennedy, Francis Schaffer, Malcolm Muckridge, and his disciple Ravi Zacharias, James Dobson, TD Jakes, Oral Roberts, Alistair Begg, Martin Luther King, Jr. & Sr., etc. These spiritual giants evangelized effectively and put their fingers in the dyke of moral decay. They served as salt and light and as prophetic watchers on the wall. They did their best to hold back the swelling tide of moral decline for decades, but in the end, the inundation was simply overwhelming. Certainly, the degree of decline has been geographical, but there remain few places in American that have been untouched. When these great men and women of God cried out, "enough is enough", they were ostracized, marginalized, maligned and belittled by the traditional church, mainstream media and new age liberals, who were more aligned with secular humanism. Maybe Jewish Rabbi Daniel Lapin described their rejection best:

"Often, as I speak on these moral issues across the country, someone in the audience hurls this tired old corker: 'The religious Right is trying to force its values down our throats.' I have a standard response which I enjoy offering. I inform my listeners that the secular Left has introduced sexual indoctrination and condom distribution to eleven-year-old public-school students. It has made the enjoyment of tobacco the moral equivalent of child molestation. It has dramatically increased illegitimacy in America. It has created an entertainment ethos that brings smut and vulgarity into our living rooms. Take an honest look at the values that the secular Left has already succeeded in forcing down the throats of religious Americans. How can anyone honestly confront the changes that have been inflicted by the secular Left and worry about the changes that the religious Right might force down our throat? I contend that the values concerned Christians desire for America are not really changes, but simply the return to an earlier and legitimate status. If you fling an invader out of your land, back over the border he illegally crossed in the first place, you are not guilty of aggression. It is called self-defense.

You are worried that the religious Right might succeed in forcing their values onto us? I am worried they might fail, for they are our values too. Or at least they ought to be." (234 words)

I know that most people, including many who call themselves Christians, are quite pleased with their liberated life style, but hopefully the following statistics will demonstrate that our nation is heading in the wrong direction and that a course correction, as Rabbi Lapin suggests, is required if America is to survive. The following are the views of Michael Snyder, author of <u>The End of the American Dream.</u>

> "The collection of facts and statistics that you are about to read is highly controversial. A lot of people are going to be greatly upset by it. Why? Because they don't like to be confronted with the truth about America. Most people tend to believe that we can "fix this country" by getting the right politicians into power or by implementing certain economic or social reforms. But the reality of the matter is that our problems go far deeper than that. A moral collapse is eating away at the foundations of our society like cancer. If it continues to go unchecked, it will inevitably destroy America. Unfortunately, fixing moral decay is far more difficult than identifying it, because it is ingrained in the hearts of hundreds of millions of individual Americans. As a society, we are decaying from the inside out, and we need to start facing the truth if we are ever going to get this turned around. If we are honest with ourselves, we see the evidence of this moral collapse all around us every day in the United States. **(182 words)**

According to Pastor Snyder's research:
- 110 million people, have sexually transmitted diseases and it costs 16 billion dollars a year to treat them
- America has the highest teen pregnancy rate in the entire industrialized world.
- There are 747,408 registered sex offenders in the US
- 89% of all pornography is produced in the US
- The marriage rate has fallen to an all-time low, more than 50% of couples "move in together" before they get married and we have the highest divorce rate in the world

- For women under the age of 30, more than half of all babies are being born out of wedlock
- One out of every three children lives in a home without a father
- More than 59,000,000 unborn have been slaughtered since 1973; 86 percent of abortions are done for the sake of convenience and 18 percent of all abortions are performed on teenagers
- 59 of all Americans believe that the traditional definition of marriage needs to be changed
- During 2012, 85,000 military veterans were formally treated for sexual abuse suffered while serving in the military
- America has the highest incarceration rate and the largest total prison population in the entire world by a wide margin.
- In America today, there are 60 million people that abuse alcohol and 22 million people that use illegal drugs.
- Abuse of prescription painkillers kill more Americans than heroin and cocaine combined.
- America has the highest rate of illegal drug use on the entire planet; the number of heroin addicts in the United States has more than doubled since 2002
- According to the FBI, there are now more than 1.4 million gang members involved in the 33,000 active criminal gangs
- 66% of all adults believe that religion is losing its influence on American life
- A study conducted by the Barna Group discovered that nearly 60 percent of Christians ages 15 to 29 years are no longer actively involved in any church

Fifty years have made a big difference in our culture! In America, just under a million legal abortions, 123,000 gay marriages and hundreds of sex change procedures occurred last year. Alcohol and drug abuse are at epidemic proportions, the murder-rate is up 300% from 2015 and more people live below the poverty line than ever before. Even though I still live in the South, the statisticians tell me that in my region, once part of the Bible-belt, 15% of us attend church once a month, 8% are LGBTQ (well above the national average), more than 60% consider themselves irreligious. So, President Obama was 100% right when he said that 21st century America is not a Christian nation. Now, do you wonder why Jesus asked the question, "will I find faith when I return"?

Abortion is killing the very soul of America. Are we so blind that we do not recognize that taking an innocent life growing in the womb is an abomination to the Creator and Sustainer of life? We must be since states have passed or are trying to pass laws to kill babies even after delivery. In fact, 3 months ago the prochoice liberals erased their 1 vote minority our state senate and we are assured that such bill will be enacted in Virginia in 2020. Governor Northam has already guaranteed it.

If there is a God and I know there is, He is deeply offended whenever we arbitrarily take a life that He designed and purposed for success. Do you think that God was napping while 60,000,000 lives have been aborted in America? If you do, you might be as surprised as were the people who lived Sodom and Gomorrah when the fire fell.

Recently, the HBO series "Chernobyl" garnered great praise. It certainly was a riveting revelation of what happened behind the Iron Curtain after a horribly disastrous nuclear accident. It portrayed Soviet people as incredibly brave and Soviet leaders as buffoons. As a historian, it gave me an opportunity to do some research on the results of the second worst nuclear catastrophe in human history. The official Soviet death count is less than 200, but it seems that there may have been 200,000 deaths over two decades, mostly caused by the fallout and contamination. The most interesting fact I discovered was that not one case of human birth defects was reported. Yet, during the 2 years following the Chernobyl explosion, 150,000 European women had elective abortions, just in case. What a travesty! Without doubt, Radical Feminism is to blame!

When I think of a woman, my wife of 51 years comes to mind. The terms that define her are caregiver, teacher, nurturer, provider, sacrifice, selflessness, commitment and love. Thanks to Radical Feminism, these words have become unflattering, even critical. Most women today want to be understood in these terms: independent, equal, accomplished, successful, determined, self-motivated, maybe summed up as, "I am woman hear me roar". At its founding in the early 1900s, the women's movement was necessary, and it accomplished many important things for women. The recent film, "On the Basis of Sex" documents those struggles. Unfortunately, like so many positive social movements, it has been hijacked by radical feminists and today a woman's right to choose has become the primary focus.

My single mother, during the period of 1947-1990, worked her way up in the rag business from a stock clerk in a small dress shop located in the rural south to store manager, the first woman in this position, for a major, nationwide, upscale department store located in a metropolitan city. She was paid more than men in the same position because she was worth every penny and she knew it. My mother was tough, determined, efficient, hard-working and a tremendous leader. Her employees loved her because she made them successful and they knew that she had pulled herself out of abject poverty and had walked in their shoes. Even though she worked long hours, she raised three son's who reflect her values and determination.

Likewise, my wife enjoyed a successful career as a teacher and principal. During the last decade of her career, over 100 employees and 750 students reported directly to her. She managed a $5.5 M budget and always ended up a school year in the black. The accomplishments of these two women could not have been possible without the women's movement. Ruth Bator Ginsberg, and others like her, sacrificed and suffered to give women equality. But the movement has gone off the rails as is evidenced by the current controversy which is allowing biological males to dominate women's sporting events, establishing new records, relegating the former holders, who are truly amazing athletes, to the trash heap. It is absurd, and harmful to women, but nothing better than this idiocy demonstrates where radical feminism is headed.

House Member Alexandria Osorio Cortez recently made a lengthy statement about Christian opposition to abortion when she said that opposing abortion should disenfranchise Christians from participating in public life. She added that abortion is an unalienable right, endorsed by most Americans, except the religious people. With the support of the largest political party, in the nation, the main-stream media and left leaning judges and justices, freedom to have an abortion seems safe in America. The Supreme Court, even the current one that is perceived to be conservative, will never overturn a woman's right to have an abortion!

So, a young woman empowered by Rowe vs Wade drives her Bimmer, displaying the bumper sticker "IT'S MY BODY", to the clinic to kill her unborn child. Her health or the health of the baby is not in peril. As with more than 90% of abortions, this horrendous crime is an act to preserve a preferred lifestyle, free from care and responsibility. Like a visit to the dentist, the unwanted tissue is removed, she drinks a Latte and returns home like nothing happened. Nothing gets under the skin of a person of faith like this kind of casual disregard for the sanctity of life. The annihilation of an innocent person, who God created in and for His glory, is akin to Hitler's morality.

For the record, an unborn child is not your body, it is incubated in the womb of the body God gave to you to nourish, protect and nurture innocent and defenseless life. A real person, capable of greatness and accomplishment, trustingly resides in you and is a sacred responsibility. There are alternatives; be unselfish for a few months, give birth to the child and then give her/him up for adoption to a family that will love and nourish this precious child. The madness must end, so the wrath of God can be appeased.

Recently, I heard Representative Ilhan Omar, tell about asking a group of girls, ages 8-12, to raise their hands if they "didn't want the government telling them when they could have babies" and that 100% said raised their hands. Although the question was obviously poorly phrased and deceptive, the girls' responses help us understand that the public schools in America are doing a great job of brainwashing our young women. The change agents, who we are paying to instruct our children, are convincing our children that the lives of the innocent unborn take second place to a woman's convenience.

Of course, the cries of women's health rings out whenever abortion is challenged. The truth is, and I know liberated women cannot handle the truth, carrying a child term is almost always best for a woman's health. If you want to talk about the 1% of cases when a woman's health is genuinely in danger, there should always be room for such exceptions. With that said, there are women who put their lives at risk every day to give birth. Many of these brave mothers do not survive, but the legacy she leaves to her newborn child is one of faith, courage and sacrifice.

The point is that the conscience of America has been seared 60 million times and now the residual scarring has made us numb to what is an obvious injustice. An abortion, at any point in the pregnancy, is viewed by most unbelievers as routine as having a pedicure. Although many Christians living through the last five decades have demanded an end to this insanity, the culture has turned a deaf ear. The only news that is reported of protest is when a fool sets off a bomb in or near an abortion clinic. The annual Right to Life March doesn't even make the evening news now.

The rights of the unborn should be the 21st century's civil rights battleground. Instead, it has become allowing confused people to use bathrooms of the opposite biological sex and letting biological men win women's sporting events; how pitiful. I am ashamed; we should all be! Even the once powerful Roman Catholic Church has lost her moral footing because of unthinkable immorality within the clergy. Now she sits in silence, shame and ignominy on the sideline as the unborn continue to perish by the millions. What a tangled web we, who were entrusted with the Gospel, have weaved. The legacy of heroes, who died for their faith with unexplainable courage in Roman coliseum, has given way to cowards who wouldn't miss a meal to defend the faith.

When the believers in Thessalonica needed clarification regarding the age when Christ would return to Earth, their spiritual leader, Paul, answered, *"The Lord shall not return until their first be an apostacy (falling away)..."* II Thessalonians 2:3a. Based upon what I have observed and continue to observe and what I see in Biblical prophecy, we have entered that stage of church history. Christianity may be all but extinguished in America by the end of this century. Christian morality, virtue and charity will be a thing of the past, as situation ethics, pluralism and relativism prevail. If Christianity does not wake up, Islam will become the dominant religion in America, especially in our major cities, where Sharia law will be enforced.

I love the America in which I grew up, but I am crushed and disheartened by the moral ambiguity that pervades society today; that which is destroying our culture and waging holy war against Christianity. I imagine that Jeremiah felt the same as he witnessed the moral collapse of the nation of Judah, under the ungodly reigns of King Manasseh and his son, Amnon. Their legacy of immorality, idolatry and human sacrifice, left the kingdom of Judah in disarray. This chaos became the inheritance of an eight-year-old-boy, Josiah.

By the time of Josiah's ascendancy, Judah had already committed such moral atrocities that God had pronounced an irrevocable curse of destruction and captivity on the nation. All that held back the wrath of Almighty God was this incredibly courageous boy king and his bold friend, Jeremiah, who was about the same age as Josiah and grew up with him in his father's court. You see, Josiah made a conscious decision to follow the God of his ancestor David, rather than gods of his father Amnon. Even as a young man, he made a sincere effort to lead the nation, which had been thoroughly paganized, in revival, repentance and recommitment to God. Unfortunately, his efforts were too little, too late. However, he was able to prepare Daniel, his three friends and an entire generation to thrive during their captivity in Babylon.

During Josiah's reign, Jeremiah began to prophesy the destruction of Jerusalem by Babylon and the captivity of the inhabitants of Judah. Josiah was spared from witnessing these horrors, as he was killed in battle when he was 39 year's old. Yet, Jeremiah lived to see Josiah's son and his Court, which included Daniel and the three Hebrew boys, taken as slaves to Babylon. He lived through Nebuchadnezzar's horrible siege and the eventual destruction of Jerusalem with the killing and/or enslavement of tens of thousands of Judeans. He wrote about the horrors and aftermath in the books of Jeremiah and Lamentations.

Could we see something like what Jeremiah lived through in America? I fear that if we continue to sacrifice our children on the altars of Moloch, we will.

CHAPTER 3 – FREEDOM OF RELIGION HAS BECOME FREEDOM FROM RELIGION

The framers/founders were religious men, and most were devoted Christians. This assertion and these men's reputations have been under assault in academia over the last three decades. Fortunately, a man of noble quality and academic excellence, Dr. David Barton, has written volumes on this topic, giving absolute proof, from the lives these heroes lived and their public and private writings, that most of the founders and framers were Christians, not Deists or Atheist's.

The same is true of the Pilgrims and Puritans who came to Salem, the Catholics who fled to Maryland, the Quakers who sought refuge in Pennsylvania and the Baptists who were forced by the Puritans to settle in the wilderness of Rhode Island. For these former European Christians, breaking away from the European model of Church-State governance was paramount in their minds. After centuries of religious wars, inquisitions and cruel martyrdom throughout the Continent, it had become obvious that religious liberty must be instituted in this new land. At the time of our founding, the Calvinists in Switzerland were still drowning Anabaptists who would not have their infants baptized in the state church, The Roman Catholic energized Inquisition was burning people at the stake and the Church of England was imprisoning and disfiguring Separatists (Pilgrims). Such practices were obviously contrary to the ideals of freedom upon which our nation was to be founded.

The Pilgrim settlers, who landed in Salem in 1620 AD, were these Separatists, who were fleeing persecution from the Church of England. Branding and ear and nose mutilation were common punishments for such "heretics" in England, so many arrived in their new home bearing the marks of their persecution. These Separatists, who fled to Holland first, came to be known as Pilgrims in the New World. They, and their more moderate cousins the Puritans, who favored 'purifying', not abandoning the Church of England, eventually established the Congregational Church in America. Congregational and Baptist Pastors led the campaign for religious freedom in the Colonies, long before the War for American Independence. Later, many served in the Continental Congress, the Committees of Correspondence and the Constitutional Convention. Adding the Bill of Rights, the first 10 amendments to the constitution, was required by many of the colonies before they would adopt the document.

The "freedom of religion" clause, included in the First Amendment, has been the most hotly debated topic in America for the last 125 years. Surprisingly, it was not so, when it was proposed and subsequently adopted. According to excerpts from the article "When the Court Took on Prayer and the Bible in Public Schools" *by* Michael D. Waggoner, published June 25, 2012, the 50th anniversary of the removal of prayer and Bible-reading from our public schools, the issued had been brewing for quite a while.

> Today marks the 50th anniversary of a court case that changed the way Americans think about religion in public schools. On June 25, 1962, the United States Supreme Court decided in Engel v. Vitale that a prayer approved by the New York Board of Regents for use in schools violated the First Amendment by constituting an establishment of religion. The following year, in Abington School District v. Schempp, the Court disallowed Bible readings in public schools for similar reasons. These two landmark Supreme Court decisions centered on the place of religion in public education. Both decisions ultimately changed the face of American civil society, and in turn, helped usher in the last half-century of the culture wars.
>
> The reaction to the cases was immediate and intense, sensationalized by the media as "kicking God out of the public school". Among America's Christian leaders, however, the response was surprisingly mixed. What was not as well known at the time, and still is not widely recognized, is that the Engel and

Abington decisions arrived on a trajectory from judicial contests and public discussions that had occurred nearly 100 years before. Today, America faces two competing, but not necessarily incompatible, realities. First, Americans speak in the secular terms philosopher Charles Taylor lays out in A Secular Age. Such secularism is neither the subtraction of religion from the public square, nor the decline of personal religious belief and practice. Rather, it is, as Taylor puts it, "a move from a society where belief in God is unchallenged and indeed, unproblematic, to one in which it is understood to be one option among others, and frequently not the easiest to embrace." Second, many scholars of religion believe that, outside of India, the U.S. is the most religiously diverse country in the world. (296 words)

A summation of this article could be, "American public schools embrace secularism in response to evidence that pluralism is the new American ideal". So, it seems that Americans have been looking for freedom from religion for 150 years; culminating with the antics of Madelyn Murray O'Hara and the ACLU 60 years ago. This leads us back to the question: What was the intended meaning of the freedom of religion clause and how was it enforced while the founding fathers survived? The answer to this question should first be viewed through their insistence of its inclusion in the Bill of Rights. The relevant constitutional text is: "Congress shall make no law respecting an establishment of religion or prohibiting the free exercise thereof...".

According to Wikipedia, the democratized keeper of American thought:

> *The Establishment Clause was derived from a number of precursors, including the Constitutions of Clarendon, the English Bill of Rights 1689, and the Pennsylvania and New Jersey colonial constitutions. From this assertion, the authors surmise, "The second half of the Anti-Establishment Clause inherently prohibits the government from preferring any one religion over another. While the Anti-Establishment Clause does prohibit Congress from preferring or elevating one religion over another, it does not prohibit the government's entry into the religious domain to make accommodations for religious observances and practices in order to achieve the purposes of the Free Exercise Clause.(98 words)*

This is obviously true in the 21st century but could not have been true in the 18th century since 99.9% of all Americans were not of "another religion", they were Christian's of various flavors. Christianity was predominant in 1776 America and the founders were not at all worried about the .1%. They were worried about America becoming a Catholic, Church of England, Lutheran or Congregational nation. They favored Christianity but preferred for each individual to be free to pick his or her own flavor.

This perspective changes everything from a historical perspective but nothing from a practical perspective. From a historical perspective, the freedom of religion clause was to prevent preference for or endorsement of any particular Christian denomination or sect. It was designed to stop the same kind of irregularities that allowed the Massachusetts' Puritans to exile Roger Williams and his Baptist followers to the Rhode Island wilderness, to stop the persecution of Roman Catholics by the Anglicans in Maryland; to legitimize and protect the hated Quakers in Pennsylvania. The Christian group that was in the majority in an area was behaving like their European cousins and that was not an American ideal. But, from a practical perspective, this bullying behavior by Christian sects in the 18th century has served to keep America from favoring any one religion throughout history. Even Satanism thrives here.

With the proliferation of non-Christian religions in America over the last 150 years, the freedom of religion clause has evolved into something of a broader scope. Please don't misunderstand; other religions deserve the same protection, but even in a broader scope, the principle is still freedom of religion, not freedom from religion. Freedom from religion is the concoction of atheists and modernists who want religion, God and the Bible completely out of the picture. In this way, they may behave in any manner they please as right or wrong is defined by the individual.

In almost every case, religion is a positive influence. As a Christian pastor, I would not object to religious texts from all the world's major religions being read in public school, along with the Bible. I have studied most of them and can say with confidence that this would be a positive, restraining, thought provoking experience, much better than total absence of any religious influence.

One thing is certain, the second part of the 1st Amendment was never intended to give us freedom from religion. Nor does current interpretation reflect the manner in which it was enforced in the US throughout the eighteenth and nineteenth centuries. Yet freedom from religion has become the mantra for secularized America, and it has been taught as the gospel in our public schools and government funded universities, which most of us attended.

An article published by the Library of Congress states so much:

The Continental-Confederation Congress, a legislative body that governed the United States from 1774 to 1789, contained an extraordinary number of deeply religious men. The amount of energy that Congress invested in encouraging the practice of religion in the new nation exceeded that expended by any subsequent American national government. Although the Articles of Confederation did not officially authorize Congress to concern itself with religion, the citizenry did not object to such activities. This lack of objection suggests that both the legislators and the public considered it appropriate for the national government to promote a nondenominational, nonpolemical Christianity.

Congress appointed chaplains for itself and the armed forces, sponsored the publication of a Bible, imposed Christian morality on the armed forces, and granted public lands to promote Christianity among the Indians. National days of thanksgiving and of "humiliation, fasting, and prayer" were proclaimed by Congress at least twice a year throughout the war. Congress was guided by "covenant theology," a Reformation doctrine especially dear to New England Puritans, which held that God bound himself in an agreement with a nation and its people. This agreement stipulated that they "should be prosperous or afflicted, according as their general Obedience or Disobedience thereto appears." Wars and revolutions were, accordingly, considered afflictions, as divine punishments for sin, from which a nation could rescue itself by repentance and reformation.

The first national government of the United States, was convinced that the "public prosperity" of a society depended on the vitality of its religion. Nothing less than a "spirit of universal reformation among all ranks and degrees of our citizens," Congress declared to the American people, would "make us a holy, that so we may be a happy people." **(282 words)**

As an educator who has been to mainland China on several occasions and was privileged to establish a private K-12 school in Huizhou, I can tell you that the Chinese government is very interested in understanding how Christianity contributed to the success of Capitalism and entrepreneurship in our nation. Most Americans, however, are oblivious of the contributions of faith to the development of our culture and have been brainwashed into making the establishment clause a different animal from that which was created. Secularists, who have controlled education and the media for the past one-hundred-fifty-years, paint the picture of a lion, when in fact the Framers meant it to be a lamb. It was simply meant to protect us from an all-encroaching state-supported Christian denomination, as was the case with Roman Catholicism in France, Anglicism in England and Lutheranism in Germany.

In Renaissance Europe, State established religions had a supreme head, the Pope, or Primate, which, except with Catholicism, was usually the King or Queen, who had absolute authority, that was enforced by the clergy and the courts. Citizens, living in countries with such state-churches, had no ability to descent or to decide not to participate. One particular brand or denomination was forced down one's throat, sideways if necessary, and religious freedom was the last thing on the mind of the enforcers. Decenters were burned, drawn and quartered, beheaded or worse. This tyranny is from what the Framers wanted to protect you and me. They were protecting us from religious tyranny, something that many who fled to America had endured.

In colonial America, .05% of the population were Jewish and .05% were other religions (Buddhist, Hindu or Muslim). The last thing these people wanted was freedom from religion, but they were thrilled with the idea of freedom of religion and the First Amendment assured that they would be protected.

When Roger Williams was forced to leave the Congregational Church and Massachusetts in 1723, a time when there was no religious freedom, he and his followers were exiled to Rhode Island and started the first Baptist congregation in America. Their persecution spoke to an outdated European idea, which was on its way out in America. Williams and his followers were not seeking freedom from religion, they were looking for freedom of religion, which was not available at that time in New England.

Now, what about President Jefferson, the supposed radical enforcer of the establishment clause? Current legal thought on the matter is based primarily on one comment he made in an obscure letter, removed from its original context. But, what we constantly are told is that he must have strongly agreed with the complete separation of church and state. Once again, we have been duped by the media as is the case demonstrated from excerpts from a Huffington Post article:

> Thomas Jefferson was criticized in his own day for his views of religion, including his belief in the freedom of religion. Mrs. Samuel H. Smith wrote a letter to him about his views. The President knew her from societal events in Washington, as well as from a prior visit to Monticello. She had heard something about Jefferson's views of religion that disturbed her, and she seems to have suggested in her letter to him that his later views are different from his earlier views. Jefferson's letter of reply is warm, but he seems to bristle slightly at times in his response. He tells her that there had been no changes, saying, "the priests indeed have heretofore thought proper to ascribe to me religious, or rather anti-religious sentiments, of their own fabric, but such as soothed their resentments against the act of Virginia for establishing religious freedom. They wished him to be thought atheist, deist, or devil, who could advocate freedom from their religious dictations." He goes on to say, "I have ever thought religion a concern purely between our God and our consciences, for which we were accountable to him...I never told of my own religion, nor scrutinized that of another... nor have I ever judged of the religion of others by their lives.... For it is in our lives, and not from our words, that our religion must be read." For President Thomas Jefferson, therefore, freedom of religion means freedom of choice.

Jefferson argued for the freedom of religion, not freedom from religion. He has been described as a deeply religious man. Would it surprise you to know that our second president, he voluntarily to be Chairman of the DC school system? As such, he required that every student have access to two books: The Holy Bible and a Hymnal. Ouch! President Jefferson also allowed a local DC Church congregation to hold services in the US Capitol Building while their burned-out building was being repaired. Double ouch! Either Jefferson was a hypocrite or has been greatly misinterpreted by those who so want to make him say what they would have preferred him to say. I think the later.

Colonial Americans were religious people, and most were Bible believers, although the Jews only accepted the Old Testament portion. Most attended church or synagogue regularly, and the federal government was not engaged in forcing the remaining 1% to follow suit. They were free to follow the dictates of their own hearts. As far as our public institutions were concerned, the Bible and prayer were included. God appeared on our money, prayer was offered at every government and public event and the Bible and prayer were welcome in public schools.

Critics will say that the 1% who were not religious were horribly offended, but there is no evidence to support such a claim. Even MMO had little support other than from the ACLU. This was the case in 1950s America. My Jewish friends or we who were from secular homes were not offended by Bible reading and prayer. It seemed to be a positive force in American life. But then, the rebel rouser in chief, Madelyn Murray O'Hair, came on the scene in the early 1960s. Newsweek dubbed her "the most hated woman in America". She fought against Bible reading and prayer like the Devil, himself. Of course, she was not on the stage alone. The liberal education system, the ACLU and the mainstream media had primed the pump for her challenges and supported her throughout her life as she continued to attempt to silence anyone, like the Apollo 11 astronauts, who dared read the Bible in a public forum. Even though the Supreme Court removed Bible reading and prayer in 1962, it took decades to clean out the last pockets of resistance. The truth is that in August 2018, a public school in Texas that proudly flew the Christian flag was finally forced to remove it.

By the way, I don't blame Mad Madeline or the others who do not want such a spiritually energized book to be read in public. The Bible self-proclaims to be an incredible change agent:

> Isaiah $^{55:11}$, "So is my word that goes out from my mouth: It will not return to me empty but will accomplish what I desire and achieve the purpose for which I sent it."

The Word of God is an irresistible force. The Great Reformer and Roman Catholic priest, Martin Luther, was converted while reading the Book of Romans. Luther had known of Christianity all his life, but he had never actually known Christ, the redeemer, until he studied the Bible. The daily Bible reading we had in elementary school was a profound influenced in my life. I will never forget my 5th grade teacher, Mrs. Desmond, praying for me with tears in her eyes. Since I lived in a secular home, the daily Bible-reading and prayer in school was the only spiritual influence I knew.

By the way, I maintain that America's spiritual decline could be halted within 6-months, if the principal of every government school in America would hire the best Bible teacher in the town and give him/her 30 minutes a day with the students. Our impressionable children are what they are because of the indoctrination they have been fed by the governmental secular humanists.

What one believes about Christianity, the Bible or prayer does not change the intent of the establishment clause; it means what it says, "Congress shall not establish state enforced religion". The Bible is not a religion. It is used and quoted by all three of the world's largest religions, which represent 80% of the world's population and it is highly respected by all other world religions. So, let's cut to the chase; it is hated by atheists, agnostics, secularists and humanists. Prayer is not a religion, although it is offered by almost every religion known to man and supposedly even 'by atheists in fox holes'. Bible reading and prayer are not religion, which is defined by Webster as "a personal set or institutionalized system of religious attitudes or beliefs."

The unanswered question that remains is – Where were the Christians when Bible reading, and prayer were removed from our schools? Why were we not out in the streets protesting, to the death if necessary? Why was there not a national boycott of the public schools? Why was a constitutional amendment not introduced?

There are three answers to these questions, the first two are quite simple, the third is more delicate:

1. Christians did not understand the scope of the decision. They failed to see that all ideas are understood through world view, so that ideas such as creationism, history, government and morality would be suppressed. We had tunnel vision and did not look beyond the 10 minutes of the day devoted exclusively to spiritual activity. We did not comprehend that since worldview controls the very way we approach learning, the

absence of moral restraint and Biblical discipline would have a staggering effect on developing minds. We did not see that in the absence of a moral standard, a new morality would fill the void, the morality of the socialist left. Today we see the outworking of this new morality that is making America less than exceptional.

2. We could not imagine that removing Bible reading and prayer would collapse the American tradition of academic excellence. The academic failure of public education in America since the late 1960s is unparalleled. The decline in SAT scores has been so drastic that ETS has had to change the test again and again and the entire scoring system to keep the severity of the decline hidden. But, here are the facts:

THE TEST SCORE DECLINE: A Review and Annotated Bibliography Brian K. Waters Human Resources Research Organization August 1981 "\; AUG 2 0 M181'" Technical Memorandum 81-2 A Directorate for Accession Policy Office of the Secretary of Defense

BACKGROUND

Beginning in 1975, the College Entrance Examination Board (CEEB) published several reports detailing consistently declining Scholastic Aptitude Test (SAT) scores over a near ten-year period. When the CEEB data were supported by American College Testing Program (ACT) data as well as an ever-growing number of achievement test score declines, educational and political forces swung into action. Over the next three years. the subject of declining student aptitudes and achievement dominated the educational and psychological literature, with many reports and books receiving heavy media and public exposure. (124 words)

What the decline in SAT scores really means
By Valerie Strauss September 14, 2011
Anybody paying attention to the course of modern school reform will not be very surprised by this news: Newly released SAT scores show that scores in reading, writing and even math are down over last year and

have been declining for years. And critical reading scores are the lowest in 40 years. (66 words)

SAT scores continue decline; 57 percent of incoming freshmen not ready for college
Eric Pfeiffer September 27, 2013
The annual SAT scores have been released to the public and show a continued decline in math and writing scores. Even worse, as CBS's Money Watch reports, more than half of incoming college freshmen are not ready for the academic challenges of college.(61 words)

SAT scores at lowest level in 10 years
By Nick Anderson September 3, 2015
Scores on the SAT have sunk to the lowest level since the college admission test was overhauled in 2005, adding to worries about student performance in the nation's high schools. The average score for the Class of 2015 was 1490 out of a maximum 2400, the College Board reported Thursday. That was down 7 points from the previous class's mark and was the lowest composite score of the past decade. The steady decline in SAT scores and generally stagnant results from high schools on federal tests and other measures reflect a troubling shortcoming of education-reform efforts. (110 words)

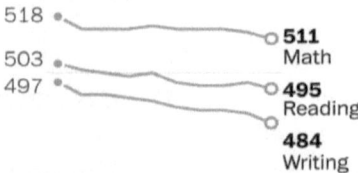

SAT scores' decline
Total group scores for the Class of 2015 were the lowest in a decade. The maximum score on each section is 800.

518
503
497
511 Math
495 Reading
484 Writing
450
Class of 2006   **2015**

Cohort data presented prior to 2007 includes students testing through March of their senior year, while cohort data from 2007 on includes students testing through June.

Source: College Board
THE WASHINGTON POST

(58 words)

And if you think the decline in SAT scores is not significant, just look at America's current educational ranking among the nations in the world.

Mathematics		Reading		Science	
Shanghai-China	613	Shanghai-China	570	Shanghai-China	580
Singapore	573	Singapore	542	Singapore	551
Chinese Taipei	560	Japan	538	Japan	547
Hong Kong-China	561	Hong Kong-China	545	Finland	545
Korea	554	Korea	536	Hong Kong-China	555
Liechtenstein	535	New Zealand	512	Australia	521
Macao-China	538	Finland	524	New Zealand	516
Japan	536	France	505	Estonia	541
Switzerland	531	Canada	523	Germany	524
Belgium	515	Belgium	509	Netherlands	522
Netherlands	523	Chinese Taipei	523	Korea	538
Germany	514	Australia	512	Canada	525
Poland	518	Ireland	523	United Kingdom	514
Canada	518	Liechtenstein	516	Poland	526
Finland	519	Norway	504	Ireland	522
New Zealand	500	Poland	518	Liechtenstein	525
Australia	504	Netherlands	511	Slovenia	514
Estonia	521	Israel	486	Switzerland	515
Austria	506	Switzerland	509	Belgium	505
Slovenia	501	Germany	508	OECD average	501
Viet Nam	511	Luxembourg	488	Chinese Taipei	523
France	495	United Kingdom	499	Luxembourg	491
Czech Republic	499	OECD average	496	Viet Nam	528
OECD average	494	Estonia	516	France	499
United Kingdom	494	United States	498	Austria	506
Luxembourg	490	Sweden	483	Czech Republic	508
Iceland	493	Macao-China	509	Norway	495
Slovak Republic	482	Italy	490	United States	497
Ireland	501	Czech Republic	493	Denmark	498
Portugal	487	Iceland	483	Macao-China	521
Denmark	500	Portugal	488	Sweden	485
Italy	485	Hungary	488	Italy	494
Norway	489	Spain	488	Hungary	494
Israel	466	Austria	490	Israel	470
Hungary	477	Denmark	496	Iceland	478
United States	481	Greece	477	Lithuania	496

Educators should be hanging their heads in shame. Rather, they are parading their new trophies: social revolution, mediocracy and innovative nothingness. So, how did removing Bible reading and prayer from public schools affect the quality of education in the classroom? I thought you would never ask.

-In the absence of brief but effective moral summary, the Ten Commandments and/or Jesus summary of the Law, "Love the Lord thy God with all you heart soul and might, and thy neighbor as thyself", social engineers and teachers have had to create and implement a system of ambiguous and constantly changing morality, culminating with the current "bathroom controversy" that now grips our nation. A Las Vegas school district has recently become the first to implement all gender-neutral bathrooms. What an accomplishment. The bottom line is that public education and our public universities are spending far too much time on ridiculous, social issues, thus neglecting vital academic curricula. That is also the case with some charter and private schools.

-Far too many teachers lack an understanding of the proper attitudes and ethics required in a profession that should model selflessness. Social agendas, indifference, insincerity and laziness grip the profession that has been redefined by the gigantic labor union, the National Teachers Association. Where once teachers were mostly concerned with student performance in academics, attitude and character, concerns now are more about working conditions, salary, input in curricula and the amount of money we taxpayers are willing to allot to our failing school systems.

-The lack of Biblical teaching and scriptural discipline in American homes has produced two generations of spoiled, confused, aimless, addicted students. Although there are still students who are motivated, aggressive and passionate about school, far too many have become ambivalent and uncommitted. To make matters worse, a recent Gallup poll demonstrated that more than 50% of four-year college graduates do not feel that their degree has relevance to their life or career. So, they and their parents spent their life savings to obtain enriched social awareness. What a waste!

3. Christians were focused on a more significant and serious issue; the civil rights movement. I will not attempt to provide a history of the entire civil rights movement, but some significant dates

are: 1954 - the Supreme Court decision to desegregate schools; 1957 – establishment of the Southern Christian Leadership Conference with Dr. Martin Luther King, Jr. elected as its first president; 1961 – Woolworth lunch counter sit-in; 1962 - first African American enrolls in the University of Mississippi; 1963 – America witnesses Birmingham police turning dogs and firehoses on marchers.

Notice that these dates were during the same period as when the Bible and prayer were booted out of our public schools. The timing created a double-barrel blow since the powerful African American Christian community and the anti-segregation white Christians were both committed to the task of ending American apartheid.

There are no figures available and they could not be trusted if they were, but I would guess that tens of thousands of African American protestors and civil disobedience participants went to jail during the civil rights years. Imagine if the civil rights issues had been adequately addressed during reconstruction, when they should have, and that the leaders in the Civil Rights Movement had been free to focus their fiery spirit of activism, courage and passion on the issue of keeping the Bible and Prayer in our schools. And I believe they would have. Had they been, Madeline Murray O'Hair, the ACLU and the secularists in government would have been in for the fight of their lives. Add white Christians, many who dared to fight for the civil rights of their African American brothers and sisters, to the mix and it would have been no contest.

So, the argument is reduced to, "Should atheists and/or secularists be forced to endure Bible-reading and prayer when it is offered?" Does the establishment clause guarantee them freedom from religion? Most Americans would answer, no to the first question and yes to the second because they have been convinced that the establishment clause was designed to protect these poor atheists from the Bible and prayer. In fact, it was designed to keep them from being required to be a member of and provide financial support to a particular Christian religious denomination. Our Christian founders understood that godlessness and moral ambiguity would only create chaos and calamity.

America has become the most pluralistic nation in the world. Every religion, including Satanism, is deemed to be equally right.

Christianity, which once dominated the American landscape, has thus been marginalized and we are paying for her absence in the complete breakdown of society. Furthermore, Christianity has become a target of the US government, its educational system and public institutions. If you don't believe it, examine the facts related to the IRS tax-exempt scandal.

The current President, Donald J. Trump, has done his very best to promote Biblical values, but for this, he has been ridiculed, slandered, impeached and made to be public enemy #1 by the left and the liberal media. This shows just how far the establishment will go to see that Christianity remains neutralized, since our Biblically based values are not aligned with their socialist agenda. Yes, America wants freedom from religion and will go to any lengths to marginalize Christianity.

This bias is also seen in the current debate between evolution and creationism. Any mention of creationism has been banned from public schools, just as teaching evolution was once banned. So, really there is no debate. The US government and its departments, institutions and fundees promote evolution and exclude creationism, yet 50% of Americans still believe that "God created the heavens and the Earth". Nothing has ever been so unjust, blatantly biased and repressive. When professors even entertain the notion of allowing creationism into the debate, their tenure is withheld, and their positions are forfeited. Government employees who dare to stand up for creationism are fired, reassigned or defunded. Christian kids who attend public-school students are ridiculed, punished and/or shunned for daring to challenge the state bias in favor of Darwin.

Evolution is the sacred cow of secularism, because it provides what American's want, freedom from religion. If the Universe, and we who inhabit it, are cosmic accidents, we owe nothing to our Creator, no allegiance, no obedience, not even a polite acknowledgement. We can live like we want or at least like the government tells us how we can live. The government is substituted as our provider, so we owe our souls to the government, not to our Creator. Convenient for tax collectors and politicians, isn't it?

This determination to neutralize Christian influence was no better seen than in the Scopes Monkey Trial. In the summer of 1926, in the sleepy little town of Dayton, TN, giants on both sides of the creation-evolution issue collided in a cosmic battle for truth. Creationism was represented by three-time democratic, populace presidential candidate, William Jennings Bryan. Evolution was represented by the infamous, agnostic criminal defense attorney, Clarence Darrow. H. L. Menken, the famous American author and cynical reporter for the Baltimore Sun, was present to heckle the deplorable Christians and cheer-on the white knight for the defense.

The issue might surprise you, for in 1926 Tennessee it was against the law to teach evolution in the public schools. That's right, the Butler Act made doing so a crime! Now before we react too harshly, let's remember that it is exactly the reverse today; it is against the law to teach creationism, even science based intelligent design theory, in our public schools.

So, as if by chance, a young substitute teacher, John Scopes, willfully violated Tennessee's **Butler Act** and was charged with teaching Darwinian evolution from an unauthorized textbook entitled **Civic Biology**, which described the theory of evolution, racial inferiority and eugenics; and the explosion ignited. The thing most people do not know is that it was all a premeditated set-up, organized and financed by the **American Civil Liberties Union** as a test case. Scopes had agreed to be tried for violating the hated Butler Act, because the regular teacher, a committed Christian, had refused to cooperate in the charade. Scopes actually encouraged his students to make notes and coached them so they could testify at the trial. They became unwitting pawns in a premeditated fiasco.

It should be noted that the expert opinions introduced by Darrow's arsenal of "experts", mostly based their support for evolution on the theory of embryonic recapitulation, an argument that has since been discredited. Yes, it was all a cleverly designed plan with an intent and purpose clearly in mind; one that brought about a 180 degree turn in the American public education system. From this point on, our courts, barraged with lawsuits, have gradually brought us to where we are today as Darwinism is the religion of choice for all government institutions.

In my last book, <u>Reconciling Genesis & Science</u>, I examine the creation-evolution controversy. If you are interested in learning more about the science supporting Creationism, I encourage you to read it. One thing I point out is that creationists do a great deal of good to improve social justice through the funding and operation of orphanages, hospitals, universities, etc.

There is a price to pay for freedom from religion. Many major cities in America are in crisis. This is the product of an amoral, God-denying culture. What is happening in Baltimoronia, my birthplace, La La Land, New Yuppie and Sanfilthsisco is unthinkable. They are worse places to live than in much of the third world. Homelessness and disease are unabated and there seems to be no end to the proliferation of crime. Lawlessness reigns supreme and now many jurisdictions have determined not to prosecute crime. The George Soros bought and paid for Commonwealth Attorney where I reside has determined not to prosecute marijuana possession, even though doing so remains a crime.

These sanctuary cities and states have taxed their middle-class residents to the point that many are fleeing, leaving only the impoverished and destitute remaining. I recently heard a brilliant philosopher say that if we do not do a better job in managing our southern border, all of America will be a third world country within 20 years. Image that!

So, if you want freedom from religion, move to China, Russia, North Korea or Cuba. Of course, you won't, because you want to enjoy the benefits of the remnants of the greatest capitalist economy in the world, left to us by the pioneers of Judeo-Christian morality and the Christian work effort. You want to have your cake (live without regards to the cultural consequences) and be allowed to eat it too. Unfortunately, the economic momentum created by these pioneers and the brave souls of the Greatest Generation will eventually dissipate as the godless socialism leads America down the pathway to destruction. Socialism, the normal byproduct of godlessness, destroys initiative, prosperity and personal freedom. Ayn Rand foretold of such a socialist collapse in her renown book, Atlas Shrugged. I guess the good news is that the destitute, wretched survivors of America's economic meltdown will have their much sought after freedom from religion.

> "And even as they did not want to retain God in their knowledge, God gave them over to a debased mind, to do things that are unthinkable." Romans 1:28

CHAPTER 4- THE AMERICAN CHURCH IS IN RETREAT

The most recent polls reveal that 15% of Americans attend church at least once a month. For contrast, 60% attended regularly in 1970. Considering the drastic decline in church attendance, over the last 50 years, the Christian church has become reactive. I walked into a large church the other day; it was more like going to the mall than to church. When I entered, pop-music was playing, there was a fantastic café, and I was able to watch the service on a large screen TV, seated on a comfy couch in the lobby as the new converts were being baptized to a Katie Perry song. This church had accomplished its goal of being a comfortable place for the unchurched. This movement of "seeker-friendly" churches is led by ARC, which has started 900 churches like this throughout America over the last decade. This model is one of four that define the American church today.

The second is the non-denominational, mega-church, which is common to most towns in America. Some of these churches are traditional while others are Pentecostal, and in many places, there is one of each. You can't miss these churches because they back up traffic on Sundays to get the people in and out of multiple services. This is where believers flock, to feel good about themselves and their faith. The worship, preaching and programs are reflective of days gone by, but that is the point. Their formula of modern, upbeat worship led by professional musicians, dynamic, non-offending preaching, exciting programs for children, teens, young adults, women and men and allowing attendees complete anonymity is ideal for those who do not want to be asked for any degree of personal commitment.

The problem is that many of the people who attend these churches are oblivious to or don't care that Christianity is losing ground. The din of activity is deceiving and anesthetizing and when one is in the company of five thousand other believers, it is hard to fathom that 85% of the people in the community aren't going to church.

I am proud to say that in my community, a gospel preaching, disciple making, straight-shootin' church is the mega. It is amazing and counterintuitive because this church and its courageous pastor is so "out of touch with the culture" that the pastor still gives altar calls, baptizes converts by immersion and has a Wednesday night service. It is part of the Calvary Chapel movement and in the communities where one of these churches is located, it is usually the mega-church. God bless all of them!

Denominational churches are the third model. Roman Catholic, Eastern Orthodox, Episcopalian, Methodist, Presbyterian, Assembly of God, Brethren, Nazarene, Church of Christ, Congregational, Seventh Day Adventists and a host of other denominational churches dot the landscape of every community in America. Contrary to the notion that denominational churches are dying, many are surviving, and some are thriving. That is not to say that through the last 25 years nearly 50% of denominational churches closed their doors, but many of those that survived have a renewed sense of mission and purpose.

Let's not forget that Catholics outnumber all other Christian churches in members and locations. During the ministries of Pope John Paul II and Benedict XVI, Catholicism thrived. The church regained her militancy in confrontation of heresy and liberalism. Many non-Catholics adored these humble servants of God, who led the renewed masses in support of traditional morality. Unfortunately, Pope Francis is not as anchored and steady as his predecessors and has unfortunately inherited a whirlwind scandal, which threatens the viability of Romanism. This recent decline in American Catholicism factors into the general malaise in which the American church finds herself.

The final retreat is the ultimate retreat. These believers, who we will describe as the Celtic evangelism movement, have abandoned the traditional church model completely. They exist in small cells, that have little form, but well-defined function. Their goal is assimilation with 21st century culture. Their proponents contend that like the Irish and Scottish tribes of the 5th and 6th centuries, they "contaminate" society with the infectious life and message of Christ as they spread throughout the land. Although leadership is informal, they have adopted a historical strategy and are hopeful of making an impact with the 85% of our culture that does not, and probable will never attend church. The church in which I am a core leader, has decided to adopt a modified model of this approach; not having Sunday service in order to serve others on Sundays and to exist primarily in small communities and service teams.

My doctoral thesis, "The Latent Romanization of the Celtic Church", which can be found at www.academia.edu., points out that although the Celts resisted Romanization, they never completely abandoned the traditional church model. Liturgy remained vitally important in Iononian churches throughout the 5th and 6th centuries Furthermore, The Synod of Whitby, in 664 AD, for the most part, conformed the Celtic Church in England, Wales and much of Ireland to Romanism. The conquest of Great Britain by the Normans in 1066 AD finished the job. It is my opinion that there is not or ever has been a "Celtic model for evangelism", but I acknowledge that the lifestyle, demeanor and daily habits of Celtic believers in that age presented an attractive, robust practical and observable faith, which can be assimilated into a model that is ideal for 21st century America. I remain hopeful for the success of this movement that is attempting to re-develop the concept of life-style evangelism. Yet, I also see how this model would be more advantageous in a post-apocalyptic setting, which may not be too far in our future if we do not heed God's warnings and repent.

I remain puzzled about why so many American churches are attempting to conform to a culture that has gone wild. Has the church ever been in lockstep with the culture? Although there are still evangelical churches that have doubled down on "that old-time religion", they are the object of ridicule and scorn by the church growth experts who want to conform to the culture. In my humble opinion there was never a reason to abandon or change what was working. It seems obvious that many Christians were so influenced by the sexual revolution that they no longer wanted their morality defined by the scriptures. An indication of that is that the divorce rate among Christians is the same as non-Christians

The Christianity I experienced when I came to Christ was not culturally adapted by any means. To be a leader in my youth group, one had to remain sexually pure, only double-date with an older more mature couple, not listen to pop music, attend church on Sunday morning, Sunday night, Wednesday night and youth group on Friday night. Girls dresses/skirts had to touch the kneecap; boys had to have short hair and we could not go to the movies. We were also asked to take our Bibles to school and be bold witnesses for Jesus.

There were not a great number of students in my high school, who attended churches like mine, but I can say that my Dutch Reformed friends made an even greater commitment to personal holiness and separation from worldliness. I can also say that we, who lived out what we might call godliness, were criticized and ostracized by other students and some faculty members. My biology teacher once told the class, "today Snowden is going to explain how a woman who never had sexual intercourse could have a baby". After I graduated, he told me that he had been expelled from Bob Jones University and had it in for "Bible-thumping hypocrites".

You may say, "this is legalism" and you would be right. Jesus said, *"If you love me you will obey me."* If that is legalism, count me in! What is wrong with having immutable standards? What is wrong with personal holiness? What is wrong with modeling godliness in a culture that has turned to godlessness? The things my future wife and I were asked to do was exactly what we wanted to do and what the Bible demands. We were both virgins when we married (through many dangers toils and snares), were extremely literate in the Word, had healthy habits regarding finances and family, and have been very happy. We have been married for 52 years and our marriage has survived many difficult trials, including the loss of our youngest son in an automobile accident when he was 17 years old. I do not regret one day of defining my life by Biblical standards and obeying my Lord, but deeply regret the days when I failed to live up to my commitments and disappointed Him.

The seeker friendly movement ignores the fact that many sinners, like me, had to go through a great deal of discomfort and personal angst to arrive at the cross of Jesus. Thank God, when I came to the point of sincerely seeking God, the church I found seemed intent on making me miserable, not comfortable. My mother, brothers and I had never attended church. We only visited Calvary Baptist Church because people from that church had knocked on our door many to invite us to attend.

When we arrived, we found that it was not "a real church", like we had expected, but a converted house, which had been remodeled as offices and classrooms. There was a large, two-story addition behind the house, in which there was a makeshift sanctuary on the first floor that seated about 100 people and four large Sunday School classrooms on the upper level. The facilities were used during the week for a fledgling Christian preschool. The buildings were not impressive at all, but the people were very friendly and welcoming. Several of the teens who introduced themselves that first day, attended the same high school as me. One young lady, who greeted us with a big smile, was to become my wife of 52 years and counting...

Pastor, Spencer Williamson, was a charismatic, southern gentleman who was impeccably dressed, fatherly, entertaining and humorous. I enjoyed the stories he told about his youth spent in Chattanooga, TN and found his sincerity endearing. I would not call his presentation polished but his message about a savior who suffered and died for me was riveting. As his sermon unfolded, I heard the clear presentation of the gospel for the first time in my life. It was like he was talking directly to me. I did not accept Christ as my Savior that day when he called for people to come forward, but seeds had been sown that others would water. Spencer was a prayer warrior and soul winner. He never met a person to whom he would not witness. Over the next 10 years, I spent hours with him praying and soul-winning, door to door.

The Pastor's son, Jerry, who served as the Associate Pastor, came to visit in our home that week. He was much different than his father; more polished, reserved and serious, but he immediately made a favorable impression on me because of his sincerity and passion. Jerry invited me and my little brothers to attend Sunday School, which we did the next Sunday. I began to attend the youth group and eventually Jerry took me under his wing and discipled me in the things of God. By discipled, I mean discipline. Jerry was God's drill-sergeant in my life and held my feet to the fire. More than any other person, he helped shape my life. Fifty-six years later, he is still my spiritual father, mentor and friend.

My two younger brothers also came to the Lord at Calvary Baptist and are both still serving the Lord today. My stepfather, an abusive alcoholic, who returned from WW II broken, emotionally gutted and angry, came to the Lord through the influence of CBC. My mother, the last holdout, gave her heart to Jesus at the age of 70 and was completely transformed by the Gospel, because of CBC. Paul told the Philippian jailer, "Believe on the Lord Jesus Christ and you shall be saved and your household". That promise came true for me and it was all stemmed from the Jesus followers who knocked on our door.

I was licensed to preach in 1970, ordained in 1973 and have been serving the Lord in pastoral ministry continually. My wife was a Christian schoolteacher, administrator and principal for 46 years. After retiring, we started an international school in Mainland China using the A Beka Book curriculum. Yet, as I approach the end of my life and ministry, I find that I am not proud of my service. To the contrary, I am disappointed and humiliated. I feel like a gangster, in a gang that has been criminally negligent for allowing Christianity to fade, Islam to surge and socialism and other forms of godlessness to take over our nation. I sense that the Lord is disappointed in me and I am disgusted with myself for not taking a stronger stand against the pagans at the walls. Now old and physically compromised, I have begun writing books to do what I can to keep serving Christ…or maybe it is my penance.

My purpose for getting so personal is to contrast my experience, and I am sure many of yours, with the seeker-friendly movement. Until recently the church had never attempted imitate the culture. For two millennia, it remained, inflexible, rigid and uncomfortably reverent. Tradition was important and Christians were not uncomfortable being called "a peculiar people". Nero burned us for light, outed us, unleashing Rome against us. Decius and Diocletian fed us to the wild beasts in the arenas, but the believers of that day died with such courage, the highest Roman virtue, that Rome was forced to end public executions. Even with such persecution, by the end of the fifth century Christianity had spread to the far-flung corners of the Roman Empire - India to Spain, Britain to Ethiopia. From 450-1970 AD, it far surpassed all other religions in number of adherents and growth rate. Although Christianity waned and wobbled throughout the Dark Ages, we made a strong comeback during the Reformation.

Make no mistake, America was founded by devoted European Christians. Many of the Separatists (Pilgrims) arrived in Salem bearing the marks of persecution, since facial mutilation was a common punishment in Great Britain for heresy. Unfortunately, the quest for money and success, caused our founders to forget the real purpose of their flight to this New World and they passed this American disease on to their descendants. But God, in His abundant mercy, sent two culture-shaking "Awakenings" to our forefathers. The Methodists, Catholics and Congregationalists moved west with the pioneers, establishing churches from Sea to shining Sea. During the 1801 Cain Ridge Camp Meeting in Logan Kentucky, classic Pentecostalism was awakened and through the 1906-15 Azusa Street Revival swept across America. Christianity was invigorated again by the interdenominational Charismatic revival in the 1960s. And, we are in dire need of a new Awakening today. What will it take to bring us to our knees?

From the time of the First Great Awakening until the 1960's, America has been blessed with the outpouring of God's spirit and favor. Unfortunately, the lukewarm Laodicean Church of the late 20th and early 21st Centuries has sought to remake itself in the image of Starbucks, Hollywood and 5th Avenue. Church growth is all the rage and Pastors are clamoring to be viewed as media superstars or maybe Christian superheroes. Dressed in designer blue jeans or $2500 suits, they spew positively focused, inspirational talks on pressing personal and social issues designed to make us feel better about ourselves and our accomplishments. We leave church supercharged for the new week, even though our lives remain fragile, broken, empty and Godless.

The conservative, orthodox preacher, John MacArthur, has compared the modern church to the ancient Laodicean church, which was located in Asia Minor:

"Government and the media, which affects the thinking of so much of America, are, for the most part, liberal and intolerant of Christianity. Leadership in both Europe and the U.S. are working for a one world government while the populace is preoccupied with their comfort and pleasure or the good life. The moral climate or condition of both free Europe and the U.S. is rotten to the core. According to a number of polls, if you compare the values, priorities, practices, and pursuits of professing Christians and non-Christians alike, you find very little difference on the whole.

The Lord Himself in the letter to the church at Laodicea warns and instructs us against the deadening and lukewarm effects of trusting in material wealth (the details of life) rather than pursuing a vital faith relationship with Jesus Christ. The Laodicean church was a church that had lost its impact on the world because it had become occupied with the world and because it had left the Lord standing outside. Whether one believes in the idea that the seven churches of Asia portray seven historical stages the church would go through or not, certainly this church illustrates conditions of the church in the 20th century in a large portion of the world."(210 words)

With this in mind, let's look at a message Jesus sent to the Laodiceans, which is found in Revelation 3:14-19:

> [14] *"To the angel (Pastor) of the church in Laodicea write: These are the words of the Amen, the faithful and true witness, the ruler of God's creation.* [15] *I know your deeds, that you are neither cold nor hot. I wish you were either one or the other!* [16] *So, because you are lukewarm—neither hot nor cold—I am about to spit you out of my mouth.* [17] *You say, 'I am rich; I have acquired wealth and do not need a thing.' But you do not realize that you are wretched, pitiful, poor, blind and naked.* [18] *I counsel you to buy from me gold refined in the fire, so you can become rich; and white clothes to wear, so you can cover your shameful nakedness; and salve to put on your eyes, so you can see."*

Jesus found two major faults with this church, and they parallel those found in many other churches of that day, especially those located in wealthy cities.

1. **Failure to be remarkable** - They were neither hot nor cold, meaning they were trying to be all things to all people. In today's church culture that means:
- abundant grace with little personal accountability
- sermons based in contemporary thought rather than the Mind of God
- enough doctrine to seem religious without ever getting to truth and
- being a little 'Churchy' without offending anyone
2. **Too self-sufficient** - The history of Christianity is one of struggle, persecution and martyrdom. Americans forget that there are millions of Christian throughout the world who find themselves in such a situation today. In contrast

to Jesus message to the Laodiceans, you may be interested in the message Jesus sent to the Church in Smyrna, which was suffering intense persecution in Revelation 2:8-11. Jesus had no criticism for them, so for churches like this, there is great hope. But, for the contemporary Laodiceans, who are blinded by their Escalades, yachts, Rolexes and Viton purses, there is only rebuke.

Wealth has served as the killer of true faith for two millennia. Christian people are giving people, not hoarders. In the founding of the Church of Jerusalem, a spirit of sharing and generosity was established. Many of the wealthy members were selling land and possessions to share with the poor and destitute members.

Similar issues were found in the church in Corinth, Greece. Paul established this church during his second missionary journey, around 56 AD. After staying there for 18 months, he departed. Not long after, troublesome reports from some of the believers in the church reached him. The Apostle Paul was forced to write a harshly worded, corrective epistle to the Corinthians and most of the pertinent issues were a symptomatic of wealth and idleness:

Sexual Immorality – A member of the Church of Corinth was in an affair with his mother, probably stepmother. This was considered immoral, even in a culture which promoted prostitution. Paul criticized their tolerance and demanded that the man be excommunicated until he repented. You may say that immorality is blind to economic status, but evidence is that the wealthy institutionalize immorality as an acceptable way of life.

Egregious Civil Lawsuits – Wealthy businesspeople tend to be in conflict. Disputes abound in complex corporate environments and Corinth had a just that. Paul took great displeasure with believers parading their problems before the "unsaved magistrates", suggesting they allow the church to mediate these matters.

Division over Personalities – I am amazed that when the Holy Spirit directed Paul to Macedonia and Greece during his second missionary journey. The first thing he and Barnabas encountered was being worshipped as Greek gods. Without an exhaustive historical exploration, suffice it to say that the Greek gods/goddesses, powerful deities created by the Titans, were like our super-heroes today, humanistic in every way. Paul put it this way in writing to the Romans, "...they worshipped and served that which was created, rather than the Creator.

This kind of humanistic pantheon thrived in more developed civilizations: Mesopotamia, Egypt, Babylon, Greece and Rome. These cultures are all closely identified with wealth, materialism, leisure and immorality. Thus, given their lifestyle and culture, the Corinthian believers had the time and passion to debate the merits and order of importance of Paul, Apollos, Peter and other mortals, who they saw as Christian gods. Of course, this behavior denies the basic tenants of the faith; humility, service and selflessness. These divisions demonstrated immaturity and lack of understanding of the basic underlying principles of Christianity, resulting from:

Failure to codify and teach doctrine – It seems that Laodicea, Corinth and the modern church did not value the two most important elements defining Christianity, doctrine and lifestyle. Doctrine provides the supportive super structure, which can only be built upon one, clearly delineated foundation. *"For God has already placed Jesus Christ as the one and only foundation, and no other foundation can be laid"* I Corinthians 3:11 GNV.

Without the right foundation, Christianity could never have survived for even five millennia. For the first 500 years of existence, the church suffered one potentially fatal, heretical assault after another, but through the unifying power of the Living Word, rightly divided (II Timothy 3:16), the "watchers on the wall" forged a consistent, sound, doctrinal super structure that sustained the true church and corrected her drift for the next 1500 years. The number of books and documents penned to define Christian doctrine would fill an ocean. The Apostle's Creed and the Nicaean Creed remain the most recognized theological statements, which define our faith.

Then dawned the 20th century, when many denominations rejected the infallibility of the Word, which provided the rivets that held the super structure together. Since then, it has been an all hands-on deck free for all. The result is that the entire concept of sound doctrine has been relegated to the past and...

> [25] *In those days there was no king in Israel: every man did that which was right in his own eyes.* Judges [21:25] (KJV)

Of course, in the absence of a doctrinal super structure held together by rivets, the Church is capable of becoming an Amoeba that can be fully adaptable to an ever-changing culture. But is that what God intended?

With the restraints of truth removed, behavior becomes conditional and situational, which has been the objective of modernism from its onset. "No shoes, no shirts, no problem". Now, that's a Christianity that fits American culture perfectly. But a church, absent of foundation (Christ), super structure (doctrine) and fasteners (the scriptures), will not survive.

On the other hand, lifestyle is the practical demonstration of sound doctrine. Jesus said, "if you love me you will keep my commandments". In another passage, he said, "the summation of the Law is to love God with all your heart, soul and mind and your neighbor as yourself." Christians who attend churches where the foundation, super structure and fasteners are intact behave in a manner imitating the life of Christ and their lives are effective in demonstrating the Gospel. I believe that most converts are at first attracted by a believer who has a contagious Christianity. As we obey, serve, pray, give and live we influence those who need Jesus.

In 1980, John Pronovost, a very successful hockey player in the NHL, joined the church in which I was serving. He had been traded from Atlanta to the Capitals. Some weeks later, I heard his testimony and it reinforces my assertion. His wife, Diane, had come to Christ through the players' wife's Bible study in Atlanta. She did not say much to him about it, but according to John, "she became a different person". Subsequently, he attended the player's bible study an gave his heart to the Lord. Diane did not have to say a word because her life screamed out the Gospel.

But now, in the 21st century, bold, innovative pastors, experts and entire movements have decided to set things straight, tear down the super structure, rebuild with "wood, hay and stubble" and their gullible, undisciplined, biblically ignorant congregants blindly follow. Jesus said,

> [15] *"Beware of false prophets who come disguised as harmless sheep but are really vicious wolves.* [16] *You can identify them by their fruit, that is, by the way they act.* [19] *So every tree that does not produce good fruit is chopped down and thrown into the fire.* [20] *Yes, just as you can identify a tree by its fruit, so you can identify people by their actions.* Matthew 17:15-16, 19-20

CHAPTER 5 – HOLLYWOOD & THE MEDIA ARE WINNING THE BATTLE OF INFLUENCE

Some acknowledge there is are genuine spiritual entities that embody evil, others say evil is a spirit or an influence and others that there is no evil at all. Yet, there is no denying that there is wickedness in our culture, and that it is supported, even promoted, by our government and the mainstream media. Abortion is the 21st century litmus test that separates Americans into two identifiable groups; those who believe that God gives life to the unborn and thus is sacred and must be protected and those who don't and consider abortion to be an insignificant removal of a lump of unwanted tissue. Today, abortion, even those done in the 3rd trimester or after birth, are looked upon by the socialist left like nothing more than the removal of a skin tag.

The pity is that since our government schools have started spending more time brainwashing our children on social issues, like women's health rights, rather than on academics, our world ranking in every academic category has plummeted, as was previously demonstrated. Unbelieving secular humanists have thoroughly permeated our schools and universities, those in the immoral left are teaching our children how to live, love and vote. The Christians who remain in the public schools are restrained from mentioning their faith in the classroom, So, why are most teachers and professors liberal? Stanford University answers that question in selected passages taken from an informative and revealing article:

> The academic profession "has acquired such a strong reputation for liberalism and secularism that over the last 35 years few politically or religiously conservative students, but many liberal and secular ones, have formed the aspiration to become

professors," they write in the paper, "Why Are Professors Liberal?" That is especially true of their own field, sociology, which has become associated with "the study of race, class and gender inequality — a set of concerns especially important to liberals." Typecasting, of course, is not the only cause for the liberal tilt. The characteristics that define one's political orientation are also at the fore of certain jobs, the sociologists reported. Nearly half of the political lopsidedness in academia can be traced to four characteristics that liberals in general, and professors in particular, share: advanced degrees; a nonconservative religious theology (which includes liberal Protestants and Jews, and the nonreligious); an expressed tolerance for controversial ideas... The mismatch between schooling and salary complements a theory that the Harvard professor Louis Menand raises in his new book "The Marketplace of Ideas." He argues that the way higher education was structured by progressive reformers in the late 19th century is partly responsible for the political uniformity of today. In the view of the early reformers, the only way to ensure that quality, rather than profit, would be rewarded was to protect the profession from outside competition. (229 words)

So, ungodly, non-believers are in control of education and public policy and they select people just like them to fill vacancies. If you have ever said, "the patients have taken control of the nuthouse", you would be right when it comes to publicly supported institutions. Thank God that there are still a handful of privately supported universities and public policy institutions for the sane and moral.

Darwinism is the official religion for our government and public educational institutions. It is the sacred cow and anyone who questions its wobbly theories are called "flat-earthers" and are destined for the mailroom. Evil stems from Darwin; it is racial bias and it devalues life. Just as the bible is the foundation of traditional morality, evolution underpins every anti-God notion that mankind can invent. Since I have already written a book, <u>Reconciling Genesis & Science</u>, on this topic, I will say no more.

The mainstream news media has become the cheerleader for everything that is antichrist: abortion, radical feminism, lawlessness, hedonism, etc. Under the mantle of the 1st amendment, they support ideas and candidates that are the farthest from Biblical morality, actually making fun of we who "cling to our Bibles" and endorse outdated, Victorian, Judeo-Christian morality. Their bold heroes are Katelin Jenner, Stormy Daniels, Hillary and Bill Clinton and George Soros, the CFO for the left. Recently, several of Hollywood's most liberal actors have said that they will no longer work with or view the work of conservatives. I would be critical if I didn't feel the same way about them. A third-party report from *Investor's Business Daily* pointed to several recent media surveys that keep proving the liberal tilt of the press, including the financial press.

> *Researchers from Arizona State University and Texas A&M University questioned 462 financial journalists around the country. They followed up with 18 additional interviews.* The journalists worked for *The Wall Street Journal, The New York Times, The Washington Post,* Associated Press and other newspapers. What they found surprised them. *Even the supposedly hard-nosed financial reporters were overwhelmingly liberal. Of the 462 people surveyed, 17.63% called themselves "very liberal," while 40.84% described themselves as "somewhat liberal. When you add it up, 58.47% admit to being left of center. Along with that, another 37.12% claim to be "moderate. "What about the mythic "conservative" financial journalist? In fact, a mere 0.46% of financial journalists called themselves "very conservative," while just 3.94% said they were "somewhat conservative." That's a whopping 4.4% of the total that lean right-of-center. That's a ratio of 13 "liberals" for every one "conservative." Whatever happened to ideological diversity? (147 words)*

Hollywood is off the chain. Their sex and violence filled films have driven audiences away and the industry is reeling financially. Cable TV has stepped up to fill the void, but they offer the very same tripe. The most popular cable television series ever is replete with nudity, graphic sexual scenes, rape and debauchery. Kerby Anderson took a reasoned look at the amount of sex and violence portrayed on television and comes away with a sobering understanding of the intensity of the problem. "From a biblical perspective, this level of consumption of disturbing images

Will I Find Faith? | 61

will result in a deadening of even Christian hearts to the clear call of Scripture to a life of purity in mind and action."

One survey found that seventy-five percent of Americans felt that television had "too much sexually explicit material" and eighty-six percent believed that television had contributed to "a decline in values." Sexual promiscuity in the media appears to be at an all-time high. A study of adolescents, ages twelve to seventeen, showed that watching sex on TV influences teens to engage in sex. A study by the Parents Television Council found that "prime time network television found that portrayals of violence are up seventy-five percent since 1998."

Deborah Fisher, Ph.D. discovered that children will be exposed to no fewer than one thousand murders, rapes, and assaults per year through watching television. She goes on to warn that early exposure to television violence has "consistently emerged as a significant predictor of later aggression." On a per-hour basis, sexual material more than tripled in the last decade. The study also found that foul language increased five-fold in a decade. The intensity of violent incidents increased significantly.

These studies provide the best quantifiable measure of what has been taking place on television. No longer can defenders of television say that TV is "not really that bad." The evidence is in, and television is more offensive than ever. Christians should not be surprised by these findings. Sex and violence have always been part of the human condition because of our sin nature (Romans 3:23), but modern families are exposed to a level of sex and violence that is unprecedented. Obviously, this will have a detrimental effect. The Bible teaches that "as a man thinks in his heart, so is he" (Proverbs 23:7, KJV). What we see and hear affects our actions. And while this is true for adults, it is truer for children.

Television's Impact on Behavior

Many studies document that what you see, hear, and read affects your perception of the world and influences your behavior. In 2000, the American Academy of Pediatrics issued a "Joint Statement on the Impact of Entertainment Violence on Children" citing over a thousand studies, including reports from the Surgeon General's office and the National Institute of Mental Health. They say that these studies "point overwhelmingly to a causal connection between media violence and aggressive behavior in many children.", The American Psychological

Association concluded forty years of research In 1992, studying the link between TV violence and real-life violence, but it has been largely ignored.

The music industry is doing no better. From hip-hop to country, songs are filled with sex and violence. Evidence is abundant that a negative impact is being made on children, teens and adults. According to the Council on Communications and Media, point out that popular music is readily available on the radio, through various recordings, the Internet, and other means, which allow adolescents to listen in various settings and situations, alone or with friends. Parents are often unaware of what the lyrics to which their children are listening to say, because of the increasing use of headphones.

Research on popular music has demonstrated its negative effects on homework, social interactions, mood swings and behavior. This research should be of paramount concern. Through the years, lyrics have become more explicit in their references to drugs, sex, and violence. The effect of music-videos are even more significant. as research demonstrates that exposure to violence, sex, sexual stereotypes and substance abuse can produce significant changes in behavior and attitudes of young viewers. With the evidence revealed in these studies, isn't it essential for teachers, pediatricians and parents to take a stand?

I really couldn't find anything good that is being said about modern media, but there is tons of criticism and warnings and many of the critics are not religious. Unfortunately, many of the artists who espouse such hedonism, practice the same. From the time of the Elizabeth Taylor-Eddie Fisher affair in the 1950's the Hollywood affair-divorce-affair-divorce train has operated nonstop. These torrid, passionate relationships have been plastered in papers and magazines and today dominate Internet content.

The same is true regarding crime, violence and sexual deviancy, but what should we expect? The vast majority of artist are amoral when it comes to their art and their personal lives. Of course, most are outspoken liberals, who spend their energy and money on saving the whales and abandoning the babies. Yet, our blinded masses keep supporting and consuming their filth.

Let me make a point that is often missed. Our criticism is of the behaviors, not directed the people. If Jesus were on earth today, He would be hanging with these actors and artists. He was often criticized by religious people for associating with tax collectors, sinners and prostitutes. He response was, "A physician is not needed by the well but by the sick." Jesus was successful in reaching those trapped in sin and giving them a new life, a second chance. One of these shady people was Mary Magdalene, a prostitute who became one of his most devoted followers. Some say she was numbered with the disciples. The point is that the the people who followed Jesus, Mary and Matthew for example, gave up their sinful professions and lifestyles. They changed their lifestyles, followed Jesus and became bold witnesses for Christ.

If today's church was more like the Church in Ephesus (Revelation 3:7-13) rather than the Laodicean Church, we believers, who are sinners saved by grace, would not be consuming trashy media, we would be out in the marketplace sharing our stories of redemption by faith and demonstrating the love of God to those in government and media who are not the real enemy. We would be praying for, loving and showering compassion to them, remembering that they have done no worse than most of us and until they encounter Jesus Christ, will continue doing what comes naturally to people who are blinded by sin.

The failure is not on the part of Hollywood, Detroit, LA, NY or Nashville, it is on me and you because we have failed to skillfully engage and reach the lost. If Jesus does not find faith in America, Christians are to blame. This is clearly demonstrated in the life of Jonah who, after a little nautical persuasion from the Lord, went to the sinful city of Nineveh, shared God's mercy and saved the city from destruction. Believers should all be like him. II Chronicles 7:14 put the onus squarely on our laps.

> *"If my people who are called by my name (Christ-ones) shall humble themselves and pray; then will I hear from heaven, forgive their sins and heal their land."*

Unless we engage, American culture will remain corrupt, and the media will remain complicit. From my perspective, this destructive influence will continue unabated until the secularist left and the socialist radicals neutralize all Christian influence.

CHAPTER 6- 21ST CENTURY AMERICA HAS BECOME 4TH CENTURY ROME

After overthrowing the Etruscan monarchy, Rome thrived for 500 years as a constitutional republic before becoming an Empire in 14 BC. From a few pastoral, Latin speaking tribes, scattered over 7 gently rolling hills in West-Central Italy, Rome grew to a juggernaut of 10 million people spread over three continents; stretching from Persia to Spain and from Egypt to Great Britain. Its governance, administration, military might, industry, infrastructure and community planning remain unmatched in human history. Rome gave civilization the arch, dome, pully, concrete, the forced march, the blitzkrieg, and the concepts of civil rights, democracy and personal freedom expressed in a republic form of government.

In 476 AD, Romulus Augustulus, the last Western Emperor, was deposed by the German ruler, Odoacer. For most historians, this marked the end of Rome, even though the Germanic peoples kept the vestiges of The Holy Roman Empire alive through the death of Hitler and the fall of the Third Reich. Some would say it is still alive today in the form of the European Union. Yet, for others, the real Rome fell in 14 BC when Consul Augustus became Caesar Augustus and the Republic died.

One hundred years before the Republic ended, Rome degenerated into a series of military dictatorships as Civil Wars, between the forces of powerful generals, destroyed the glory of the Republic. Eventually Julius Caesar, Great Uncle of Augustus Caesar, emerged as the victor. Brutus and other Senators assassinated him in an attempt to save the Republic, but in the aftermath of his death, young Augustus became Rome's first Emperor and the dream of freedom died.

Why did the mighty Roman Empire fall 464 years after its inception? Below is my feeble attempt to unravel the greatest mystery of the ages, which is taken from my book, Foundations of Western Civilization from a Christian Perspective.

BACKGROUND

In 410 AD, the Goths led by King Alaric, breeched the walls of Rome, invaded and looted the city. Because the Goths he led had accepted Christianity through the missionary efforts of Ulfilis, they spared the churches when they sacked the city. Since churches functioned as archives, much of the knowledge and writings from the ancient world were saved. This merciful act was vital to the survival of western scholarship through the Dark Ages. It is through these documents that we have such a clear picture of the inner workings of Rome throughout her history. A few years later, the Huns invaded, then the Vandals each tribe sweeping across Rome's shrinking northern border. Finally, a terrible plague hit the city.

In just over a century, the population of the City of Rome declined from nearly one million to fewer than 80,000 people. Nine out of ten citizens had died from plague, famine, by the hand of the invaders or had fled from Rome entirely. By the time the first Germanic Caesar, Odoacer, ascended the throne, what the Germans inherited was a mere shadow of the great Roman Republic. Thereafter, a succession Germanic princes took the title of Caesar, later changing it to the German title Kaiser. but the Latin Roman Empire was gone.

One hundred years later, the Byzantine (Eastern Roman) Emperor, Justinian, re-conquered Italy, Spain, North Africa and other parts of the old Western Empire. Justinian's reign is marked by the ambitious but only partly realized renovatio imperii, or "restoration of the Empire". Because of these restoration activities, Justinian has sometimes been called the "Last Roman". This ambition was expressed by the partial recovery of the territories of the defunct Western Roman Empire from the Goths and Vandals. His general Belisarius swiftly conquered the Vandal Kingdom in North Africa, extending Roman control to the Atlantic Ocean. Subsequently Belisarius, Narses, and other generals conquered the Ostrogothic Kingdom, restoring Dalmatia, Sicily, Italy, and Rome to the Empire after nearly a century of barbarian control.. He is also known for 'Justinian's Code', a reorganition Roman law in an orderly and scholarly manner, and the construction of Hagia Sophia Cathedral in Constantinople. Upon his death, however, the west entered a period known as the Dark Ages.

It has been said that Rome fell from within before it fell without. Millions of words have been written on the subject; yet, I hope that this brief summation does justice to the scholarship of so many great men and women who have attempted to make sense of it:

1. Power Corrupts and Absolute Power Corrupts Absolutely – Most scholars would argue that Caesar Augustus, the grand-nephew and heir of Julius Caesar, was a benign ruler. Certainly, vestiges of the Republic remained, and Augustus was careful to not exclude the Senate and Tribunes in governing. The same might be said of his stepson Tiberius Julius Caesar, but none could argue that for Tiberius' nephew Caligula, Claudius or Nero. They were virtual monsters, who ruled with an iron rod. Ruling as absolute despots, they brought about mayhem, corruption and barbarianism. The next 500 years featured "Five Good Emperors" (98-180 AD), a host of hacks and far too many maniacal goons drunk on power, sex and wealth.

   Even the Emperors that are considered "good" struggled with maintaining the Legions in the face of declining nationalism and ambiguous morality. For instance, both Hadrian and Trajan built walls that redefine and pulled back the northern extent of Roman control in Britain. Eventually the weakened Empire was forced to completely abandon their northernmost prize.

   Upon the death of the last good emperor, Marcus Aurelias, Commodus, one of the worst Emperors ever, shipwrecked Rome. He was greatly unpopular, so in order to curry favor he distracted the populous with an extended series of extremely bloody gladiatorial games. At the games he distributed loaves of bread (dole in Latin) to attendees. If you are missing the point, the people were able to attend the games because there was no work available in the collapsing economy and they learned that government, not their own initiative and determination, was their provider.

   Later, with chaos ascending, both Diocletian and Constantine foolishly divided Rome into separate administrative districts to try to manage an out of control bureaucracy. Constantine went as far as to make Constantinople the Eastern Capital of the Empire, further weakening the west. Long after the Western Empire collapsed, the Eastern Empire thrived. Emperor Justinian reconquered most of Rome's former territory in the West, but he could not maintain control of it. The church in the East, which would become the Eastern Orthodox Church, provided a continuity of faith and tradition that allowed the Eastern Empire to survive until 1453 AD.

2. Weakening of the legions - The 5th-century Roman historian Vegetius, believed that the military fell from within. As the lack of discipline increased, Legionnaires stopped wearing all their protective armor. This made them vulnerable to arrows, which at times caused them to flee the battlefield. Overconfidence and lethargy also led to a decline in rigorous drilling. He also blames the decline in the quality and commitment of the officers, who motivated troops through bribing them with booty rather than through their pride in Rome. This indicates that nationalism was in decline.

At one time serving in the army was the cherished duty of every citizen. Before the Civil Wars that destroyed the Republic and the ascendency to an Empire, Romans were proud of their heritage, language, culture, inventions and strength. It truly meant something to be a Roman and every citizen understood that he or she owed a debt to Rome. After the republic ended, the value of citizenship responsibility seems to have declined. This directly affected the strength of the Legions.

Even those who were not citizens hoped to become so through military service. But much damage was done to the image of the Legions during the civil wars which took place in the last century before Christ. The greed and avarice of the soldiers resulted in loyalties more to their Generals than to Rome. Over time, as Romans got softer, military service became a burden not a privilege. Wealthy Romans began to pay lesser men to serve their military obligation, which led to further decline in the legions. History teaches us that fewer men with clear objectives, good training and advanced technology can overcome armies with greater numbers.

By the end of the 4th century, half the Roman army was composed of Germanic soldiers, who had no loyalty to Rome whatsoever. We are reminded in history of the German mercenary troops (Hessians) who fought for the British, against the American patriots. They were feckless, indolent and inconsequential. There was a time when Rome's legions were feared throughout the civilized world, but as that changed, the Empire became indefensible. Simply put Rome lost its military edge and the Germanic and Hun invaders took advantage of this weakness.

During the final century of the Western Empire, the Germanic tribes penetrated Rome's northern border. As they drew nearer and nearer, a treaty was initiated that allowed them to live in and farm the northern frontier. Under mounting pressure from the Huns, the Romans hired the Goths to defend the Empire's territory in the north. Once the Huns had been temporarily repelled, the Visigoth King, Alaric, invaded and sacked Rome in 413 AD. After that, the Huns, the Vandals and a host of others invaded Rome at will and the Roman Legions were powerless to stop the invading hordes.

3. Decline in the Economy – The resources required to support an agrarian nation that stretched from Spain to Persia and from Britain to Carthage was incredibly complex. Others like Sumer and Egypt had failed before and were subsequently conquered. Over time, as the Empire languished, the interdependent components of such a complex economy became unsustainable.

Rome's natural resources had been exhausted from generations of use and abuse. Taxation became so burdensome that industry and personal initiative were crushed. Far too many people, especially farmers, were "on the dole", a term describing the masses who depended on free loaves of bread which were distributed daily by the Emperors to gain popularity. The cost of sustaining a world controlling military was far too great. Balance between imports and exports were upset as Romans became consumers rather than producers.

As a result of the Civil Wars and the Marian Reforms, much of the best farmland throughout the Empire was taken from the citizens and given to soldiers. Roman farming declined as these soldiers and their descendants were unable or unwilling to invest in the land and work hard to make a profit. Eventually, most farms became collectives and/or went to ruin.

Without a robust agricultural component, the value of almost all goods declined, forcing the middleclass merchants and traders to fail. The value of money plummeted, and the economy collapsed. This left a binary system comprised of the very rich, who were not affected, and the very poor, who could no longer pay taxes to support the governmental and political system.

4. Decline of the Family Unit and Traditional Roman Morality – Rome was built upon strong nuclear families. During the days of the Republic, the family unit was supreme. Entire families shared a villa (from which we get village), a series of homes clustered together. The eldest male ('Paterfamailis') led their families as they worked together to carve out a better life. Sacrifice and hard work were expected from every family member. Historians have noted that the Roman family reflected the principles that would come to shape Rome's republic.

Although the beginning of the decline in Roman values began with the corrupt Third Punic War, the coming of the Empire brought a rapid decline in moral standards and family unity as the elites in power flaunted all semblance of morality, good governance and family values. Seeking pleasure through recreation, gladiatorial games and brothels, growing slave abuses and a lack of respect for the elders accelerated moral decline and caused Rome to lose what had originally made them strong.

Divorce was almost unknown in the early Republic, but it became more common after the era of the Civil Wars and proliferated in the era of the Empire after Caesar August forced his stepson Tiberius to divorce his wife in order to embrace a more advantageous political marriage. This principle, known as "affectio martalis", became more and more prevalent. Before long, marriage vows meant nothing, and the blended family became predominant. These families were less structured and lacked the discipline of the nuclear family. As the family unit goes, so goes the nation.

It took Christianity nearly 400 years to be accepted by Rome. Paul visited the city around 60 AD, tradition says that Peter visited some years later. According to Paul's letter to the Church in Rome, there were "members of Caesar's household" that had become Christians. Nero destroyed any chance for the new faith to take hold as he blamed Christians for burning Rome and executed Peter and Paul. Some years later, the Roman Governor of Bithynia, Pleiny, wrote a detailed letter to the Emperor to inform him that Christianity was not a Jewish sect, but was mostly comprised of Greeks and Romans. This increased the persecution. During the period 250-305 AD, Christianity suffered its most intense pressure ever as the Emperors Decius and Diocletian decided that the expansion of Christianity was robbing Rome of her power and might. Diocletian's horrible persecution ended abruptly in 305 and nine years later, Christianity was made a legal religion by Constantine, who took the opposite view of his predecessors.

Christianity helped restore some moral sanity late in the Empire but by that time the damage had been done. Furthermore, the Church was actually weakened by the influx of unconverted soldiers and bureaucrats, who became christians in name only to please their Emperors. In fact, most of the doctrinal grievances that brought about the Protestant Reformation, were initiated during this initial period of Romanism. There is no doubt however that the church provided the stability the conquered Romans needed to make the transition from being the masters to servants and it eventually converted all of the Germanic tribes, who established the Revived Roman Empire under Charlemagne in 800 AD.

CONCLUSION

From Rome's fall we should learn that a republic is the superior form of democracy and the nuclear family is the superior environment in which to train children who contribute positively to society. After the rise of the Empire, Roman laws were primarily enforced for the good of the Emperors and the state. After the Renaissance, democratic republics throughout Europe and in North America would come to understand that government is for the good of the governed.

The protection of Roman law and civil rights were never extended equally throughout the Empire. Citizenship applied only to a select group who were granted liberal civil rights. The New Testament lists several occasions in which the Apostle Paul, a Syrian Roman citizen, enjoyed the benefits and protection of the law, while other of the Apostles did not. The republic had certain 'built in' protections for even the common Plebeians, but many of the Emperors disregarded them. Most of the emperors were despotic, selfish, power hungry, cruel, even mad. That kind of leadership can only produce failure. So, the internal fall of Rome led to the external fall of Rome and we as history students must learn from Rome's mistakes.

PROLOGUE

The left will continue to perpetuate the myth that Rome fell from lead poisoning in their water and cooking vessels. This makes it much easier to confuse the millions of students who get the revisionist version of history from public schools filled with the unsubstantiated notions of left leaning socialists like Howard Zinn. A Peoples History of the United States is a prime example of the tripe that is being fed to an unsuspecting and naïve generation, whose parents were blinded to the truth by the very same propaganda in the public universities they attended. If you sincerely want to know the truth about our founders, look to primary source documents, which are readily available.

Let's remember that every civilization mentioned in this book, no matter how great, is gone. The Roman civilization lasted a millennium; these United States are just over 240 years old. It may be that this generation will determine the fate of this great land. The purpose of this book is to provide a pathway for you who will objectively investigate the past to obtain a clear vision for the future. Remember those who do not learn from the mistakes of history are destined to repeat them.

Franklin Graham, Paula White and a host of Christian leaders see a ray of hope for the salvation of America emerging in the form of Donald J. Trump. Their hope is well supported since he has: passed unprecedented criminal justice reform, appointed two anti-abortion Justices to the Supreme Court and scores of others to lower federal benches, stimulated the economy and generated millions of new jobs, unprecedented numbers for African and Hispanic Americans and women. Through reducing regulations, he has made the US energy self-sufficient, revived the Rust-Belt states, restored pride and hope to neglected communities, led in the elimination of the individual mandate from the ACA, the most egregious part of Obama Care for Christians, has stood steadfast for Israel and reenergized the pro-life agenda and traditional family values.

Since President Trump openly and aggressively promotes Christian values, he is treated like the rest of us "deplorables" by the left and liberal media. I wonder if he will even be reelected in the fall. In the aftermath of the 2018 election, the President's party lost 41 seats in the House of Representatives. The radical left has rallied, upped the ante for their anti-American agenda and are going to new extremes to secure their liberal, socialist positions. Several state legislatures have adopted abortion on demand for any time during pregnancy and some allow the murder of the newborn infant after delivery. The President has been impeached by the House and the media is in a feeding frenzy. Members of Congress and the media are comparing him to Hitler and there seems no end to how far they will go to obliterate him from the pages of history. Currently, he is trailing most of the democrat candidates in the polls for the general election in November. And as this manuscript goes to the publisher, a new virus is being reported in China that could become a pandemic and threaten our economy.

I hope and pray that President Trump will be reelected, as long as he continues to be influenced by the Christian leaders who are close to him, like Mike Pence. The VP recently mentioned that the President often asks cabinet members and others in the White House to pray for him. We all should pray for our President! Bible loving Christians, conservative Jews, capitalists and blue-collar workers love the President, but the academic community, media, elitists, secular humanists, socialists, Never-Trump republicans, radical African Americans, Millennials, illegal immigrants and the liberal clergy hate him. The degree of polarization in our nation has not been so intense since the Civil War.

Unfortunately, I fear that far too many Americans want no part of a Godly culture and prefer to remain in a marijuana stupor and live their lives as Epicureans. Bill Marr, Michael Moore and other celebrities have openly said that they are hoping for a horrible recession so Trump will not be reelected. I wonder if Trump's enemies are doing more than hoping; is it possible that they are developing a strategy to cause such a recession? My wife and I lost our home and most of our retirement portfolio in the 2008 crash, as did millions of others. It is hard to believe that there are people so callous as to want to put us through something like that again, just to rig an election.

I also pray that the hopelessly lost Christian church will stop the gimmicks and go back to preaching the Gospel and making disciples. Wouldn't it be wonderful if Americans would begin to cry out to the Lord in repentance and faith? There is anecdotal evidence that this could happen, from what occurred, just after the 9-11 catastrophe in 2001. During this period, our nation experienced an incredible religious awakening. I witnessed it first-hand. On the first Sunday after the disaster, our church attendance was up by 50%. I am told this is what happened in most churches. The increase was split evenly with casual participants who rarely attended and new people who were seeking solace. The mood was somber, many people were tearful and there was a sense of repentance in the air. We had a tremendously moving and impactful service and it ended with hundreds of people coming to the altar to receive or make a fresh commitment to Christ. The surge declined about 20% each week, until by the 5th week everything was back to normal.

This spontaneous mini-reawakening came from an event that lasted 4 hours and claimed three-thousand lives in two isolated locations in America. No doubt, it was visually and emotionally impactful on the entire population, but outside of Manhattan and Washington, DC, a relative few individuals experienced extreme loss, pain and suffering. I wonder if an event was repeated on a nationwide scale, that took millions of lives and destroyed or crippled the infrastructure that makes America work, would the response be greater and more sustained than it was from 9-11? Unlike Bill Marr, I would never wish such a tragedy on our great land, but there are many who are saying that if our nation does not repent, we will face the judgement of Almighty God.

If there is any real hope, it is in the potential of the remaining genuine, wholehearted believers who are praying and humbling themselves in the face of intolerable treatment by the socialists, deep state and media. As pointed out previously, national revival and reform begins with "My people, who are called by My name". No one can predict the future, but God is in control as He was in the days of Jeremiah. In that case, during the reigns of Manasseh and Amnon, the Jews had offended God so terribly that Isiah and Jeremiah prophesied devastating judgement upon

Jerusalem and the Jews. King Josiah, son of Amnon and a contemporary of Jeremiah, was determined to serve the God of his ancestor David. In a last-ditch effort, the young King made an attempt to bring the nation of Judah back to God, but it was too little too late. However, Josiah was able to bring about a generational revival that prepared Daniel, his three friends and tens of thousands of Jews for life in captivity, bondage and slavery in Babylon and Jeremiah was able to give a message of hope for the future of Judah. Because of God's boundless mercy, the Persians who conquered Babylon allowed surviving Jews to return home and rebuild Jerusalem seventy years after their captivity began. The truth is, that the people who returned were more spiritual and obedient to God, than their forefathers. Thank God for the ministries of a Godly political leader and a faithful prophet.

America has been "a pot of gold in the hand of the Lord". We have sent and financially supported tens of thousands of Christian missionaries, who have encircled the world with the Gospel. We have defended the world from aggression, terrorism and cruel dictators. We neutralized Godless socialism in Russia and Eastern Europe. We have favored Israel and have cared for the world's refugees and disenfranchised. Surely, the gracious Lord will remember us and restore us before it is too late.

I want to have hope for the future of this great nation but must acknowledge that it would take a miraculous revival. For that miracle to happen, **God's people** would have to:

- humble themselves and pray
- reject lukewarm Laodicean churches and embrace churches that preach the gospel of repentance and faith and produce steadfast, committed disciples
- have the courage to suffer intense persecution from the socialist left
- recommit to our spouse and children and restructure our families to a Biblical model as is referenced in Ephesians 5 and Colossians 3
- completely renovate government schools or homeschool our children using a Christian curriculum (A Beka, Veritas, Bob Jones Press, etc.) or enroll them in a Christian School that refuses federal money and is committed to helping families produce deeply devoted Christian young adults

- place our older children in thoroughly Christian or radically conservative colleges or universities
- stop watching and listening to media garbage that pollutes the mind and the soul
- study and obey the Bible, individually and as families
- become missionaries in post-Christian America and share the Gospel with those lost in a sea of confusion and corruption
- reach out and give a helping hand to the poor, hungry, homeless, confused and discouraged
- work for and contribute to morally conservative candidates who oppose abortion, infanticide and all forms of godless socialism
- challenge those who call evil good and good evil; point out their folly in love
- be bold about our passion for God and our nation's founding documents
- refuse to be silenced by the mob; in other words, become a martyr

Remember that America is just our temporary residence. Be inspired and encouraged that eternity offers the hope of perfect justice with the absence of sin, sickness, death and sorrow. And, if America fades God is still in control and will use another emerging Christian nation to carry the banner of truth to the rest of the world.

Unfortunately, the tide is against us! Liberalism, socialism, godlessness and evil have gained the advantage and with

- every student who enters public schools
- every high school graduate, even those from sound Christian homes, who enrolls in a public university
- every divorce or family separation
- every tax dollar that goes to Planned Parenthood and then back to leftist candidates
- every radical African American leader who vilifies the innocent for the sins of their ancestors
- every anti-American radical, who wins a seat in Congress
- every new film, song or TV program that promotes hedonism, devalues the family and marginalizes the accomplishments of our heroes from the past and present

- every socialist that offers and promotes government programs as a substitute for rugged individual accomplishment
- every Millennial who determines that it is a priority to save whales and kill the unborn
- and every church that marginalizes the Gospel by not preaching repentance, salvation by faith and unconditional obedience to the Word of God

Christianity is in crisis and America gets closer to insignificance and quietly disappearing from the pages of history or of falling into the hands of a just God. Paul told us, "When you have done all that you can do, stand". Ephesians 3:16.

Who will stand for righteousness?
Who will stand for Biblical families?
Who will stand for the unborn?
Who will stand for those trapped in confusion, caused by a culture that is out of control?
Who will stand against ANTIFA and the socialist mob?
Who will stand to protect our children from predators?
Who will recommit every ounce of life, breath and soul to restore America's Christian virtue?
Who is willing to give their last full measure of devotion to the nation that has given us life, liberty, and the ability to pursue happiness?

> *"But if serving the LORD seems undesirable to you, then choose for yourselves this day whom you will serve, whether the gods your ancestors served beyond the Euphrates, or the gods of the Amorites, in whose land you are living. But as for me and my household, we will serve the LORD."* Joshua 24:15

It is your choice. If you are ready to follow Joshua's example, there are millions of others who are willing to stand with you. Please reach out to us on this book's Facebook page.

www.ingramcontent.com/pod-product-compliance
Lightning Source LLC
LaVergne TN
LVHW041538060526
838200LV00037B/1040